THE
REVELATION
OF
JESUS

TEACH Services
Brushton, New York 12916

Scriptural references taken from the New International Version unless otherwise noted. Permission granted from the Zondervan Corporation.

Library of Congress Catalog Number 90-70482

ISBN 0-945383-18-5

Published by

TEACH Services
182 Donivan Road
Brushton, New York 12916

Wake Up America Seminars, Inc.
P.O. Box 292584
Dayton, Ohio 45429

Ordering Information

If you wish to purchase additional books to obtain or complete a set, please indicate which volume(s) you would like to have and the number of each book you want. Make check payable to: Wake Up America Seminars. Allow 2 to 4 weeks for shipping.

"The Revelation of Jesus" Volume I $12.00

"The Revelation of Jesus" Volume II $12.00

"The Revelation of Jesus" Volume III $12.00

3 Volume set $36.00*

Volume discounts are available.

* Books can be mixed if necessary, it is not necessary to purchase complete sets. Add 10% for sales tax and shipping per order.

Acknowledgements

To all who are anxious for the immediate return of Jesus, this book is dedicated.

Deepest appreciation is due to my wife and daughter for they granted me thousands of hours to prepare these volumes. Even more, my wife consented to take full time employment so that I might resign from my job to proceed with this work.

Special thanks is due to many dear friends who helped to make these books a reality.

"The Revelation of Jesus"

24 Bible Studies On Coming Events

Volume 1

Volume 2

Volume 3

Preface

This second volume builds on the premise that gospel truth is ever unfolding. God's Word is not motionless or dead. New elements within the plan of salvation continue to emerge just as new discoveries surface in other sciences. While it is true that major discoveries may not happen every decade, the point is - they do happen. This author believes a final discovery is taking place within the Bible that will over-shadow all technological marvels of the 20th century. I believe Revelation's mystery is beginning to break open!

Those who study prophecy search the deep things of God. The very nature of the subject calls for a certain amount of trepidation and wonderment. Those who seek understanding on this subject must navigate carefully and thoughtfully. The temptation to jump to a hard and fast conclusion is almost overpowering. Even though the student must be persistent in his search for harmony from the sum of prophetic parts, he must never close his mind to new issues or views.

If the mystery of Revelation's story can be understood, then any claim to know what Revelation says raises an enormous problem. How can an interpretation be proven true or false? Logical deductions are not good enough. (For example, the flat-world theory was very logical for thousands of years.)

There are two ways to test an interpretation. First, time will tell. If a prophetic interpretation is true, i.e., if it faithfully represents the meaning of a prophecy, a clear harmony should be found between the inter-pretation and the predicted event. People having different religious backgrounds should be able to investigate the parallel between an interpretation and the event claimed to be a fulfillment to see if harmony exists. If the predicted event confirms the interpretation, a fulfillment has occurred.

But what about things that haven't happened? The second and equally important component in validation is internal. God does not remove the possibility of doubt. He did not send a shower or two before Noah finished building the ark to impress people that water **could** fall out of the sky. God does not put Himself on trial. Rather, He provides reasonable evidence to legitimize the claims of His servants. As the animals arrived at Noah's ark in pairs and sevens, it should have been obvious to the scoffing observers that this was no ordinary event. How could the animals have known it was time to get in the ark? God will not overwhelm anyone with evidence if they choose to ignore or reject what He has given. This is why Revelation says seven times, **"He that has an ear, let him hear what the Spirit says..."**

Prophecy leads us to the conclusion of the plan of salvation. The plan of salvation is larger than man can understand. It is as profound as it is simple. It is more complex than anything man-made. It is more majestic than anything composed by man. It is far more enclusive that any human heart can reach.

Those who attempt to understand the plan must personally wrestle with God. This is where most Christians fail. It is not enough to understand or accept the plan for personal needs - as essential as they may be. If we are going to appreciate Jesus for the God He really is, we must attempt to comprehend something about the height and depth of His love. We must put His love into this perspective: Jesus is returning to earth and earth presently contains 5.2 billion living people. Who will He take to heaven?

Larry Wilson

January, 1990

What time is it?

Part I

Lesson 7

Review

Our last study surveyed the sweeping prophecy of Daniel 2. King Nebuchadnezzar's dream concerning the kingdoms of man has almost been fulfilled and historical confirmation brings the fulfillment of the vision down to our day. But what time is it? Will there be 100 more years before Jesus returns? Are we really living in the last days? If we are, how is it proven?

There is only one prophecy in the Bible that tells us where we are in time. Other prophecies like Daniel 2 and Daniel 7 tell us where we are sequentially but only one leads us to a specific date so that we may know our chronological position. It's found in Daniel 8-12.

Introduction to the prophecy

1. This prophecy is directly connected with the work of Jesus in the heavenly sanctuary.
2. This prophecy has five very important dates connected with it. All five dates have been historically confirmed.
3. Unlike the first seven chapters of Daniel, this prophecy is written in Hebrew.
4. This prophecy came to Daniel in segments over a period of about three or four years. The last five chapters of Daniel (8-12) contain this prophecy.
5. Even though a portion of this prophecy applies to Daniel's day, the focus is the "appointed time of the end."

The Vision

Sometime during the third year of King Belshazzar's reign (last king of Babylon), Daniel received the first segment of this serious vision. A summary of Daniel's vision follows:

---

1. I was standing beside the Ulai Canal... Before me was a ram with two long horns standing beside the canal. One of the horns was longer than the other but grew up later. I watched the ram as he charged toward the west, north and the south. No animal could stand against him... He did as he pleased and became great. {v1-4}

2. As I was thinking about this, suddenly a goat with a prominent horn between his eyes came from the west, crossing the whole earth without touching the ground. He came toward the two-horned ram... and charged at him with great rage. I saw him attack the ram furiously... and shatter his two horns. The ram was powerless to stand against him; the goat knocked him to the ground and trampled on him. {v5-7}

3. The goat became very great, but at the height of his power his large horn was broken off, and in its place four prominent horns grew up toward the four winds of heaven..." {v8}

4. Later, out of the four winds, another horn arises. It starts small, but grows in power to the south and east and toward the Beautiful Land. It grew until it reached the host of the heavens, and it threw some of the starry host down to the earth and trampled on them. {v9-10}

5. This horn sets itself up to be as great as the Prince of the host; it takes away the daily sacrifice from him, and the place of his sanctuary was brought low. {v11}

6. Because of rebellion, the saints and the daily sacrifice were given over to it. It prospered in everything it did, and truth was thrown to the ground. {v12}

7. At the end of this vision, Daniel heard two angels talking as he watched this vision. One angel asked five questions {v13}. They are:

a. How long will it take for the vision to be fulfilled?

b. How will the daily be taken away?

c. How long will the rebellion that causes desolation last?

d. How long will the sanctuary be surrendered?

e. How long will the people of earth be trampled upon?

The vision has two parts

During the vision, the angel Gabriel was sent to Daniel with the instruction, "tell this man the meaning of the vision." As will be seen, the content of the vision is so comprehensive, that Gabriel actually requires three visits to give Daniel a full explanation! The first visit of Gabriel begins in Daniel 8:15. Before explaining the vision to Daniel, Gabriel twice emphasizes that this vision concerns "the appointed time of the end" (verses 17 and 19). The visit of Gabriel with Daniel took place about 25 centuries ago. Several times in this vision the phrase "the appointed time of the end" is used. The phrase leads us to believe that God must have an appointed time to end the troubles of earth. Are we living in the last century? Have we reached "the appointed time of the end?" How can we tell if we have or haven't? Just as a navigator looks at the stars to know his latitude and longitude, there has to be some sign or event that shows our chronological position in time so that we can know when the appointed time of the end arrives. Without a marker, we can only guess at the time.

Many people challenge the idea that we are living at the end of the world's history. They ask, "what evidence do you have to show that the end is now and not 500 years from now?" The world has seen WW1, WW2 and there will be a WW3 (according to Revelation). So how can we know that we are living at the end of the world? Bible prophecy holds the answer. Jesus has declared the end from the beginning. Gabriel told Daniel, **"...none of the wicked will understand, but those who are wise will understand."** Daniel 12:10

Even though the vision of Daniel 8-12 serves a variety of purposes and answers a number of questions, it basically has two parts. The first part establishes a historical footing or marker so students of prophecy can determine their chronological position from historical sources. The second and more complex portion of the vision explains certain events that occur during the appointed time of the end. It is also important to know that other prophecies in the Bible add information to compliment the vision of Daniel!

The explanation begins

In his first visit with Daniel, the angel Gabriel said:

1. The two-horned ram that you saw represents the kings of Media and Persia. {v20}
2. The goat is the kingdom of Greece, and the large horn is the first king. {v21}
3. The four horns that replaced the one that was broken off represent four kingdoms that will emerge from this nation but will not have the same power. {v22}
4. Later, (during the appointed time of the end) when lawlessness has gained control of the world, a stern-faced king, a

master of intrigue, will arise. He will become very strong, but not by his own power. He will cause astounding devastation and will succeed at whatever he does. He will destroy the mighty men and the holy people. {v23, 24}

5.   He will cause deceit to prosper. He will consider himself superior and when the world feels secure, he will destroy many and take his stand against the Prince of princes. Yet he will be destroyed, but not by human power. {v25}

Commentary

Some commentators separate the last five chapters of Daniel into a number of unrelated visions because it is obvious that the visions and explanations come to Daniel over a period of time. However, we will see that each time Gabriel talks with Daniel, he refers to one of their earlier visits and/or a portion of the vision seen earlier. This clearly demonstrates a unity between the segments. Further, if we tie the five chapters together, the pieces will harmoniously relate to each other. If the vision is broken into disconnected parts, conclusions will have no historical footing to work from. In such a case, the appointed time of the end cannot be determined. We will see that Jesus carefully tied the historical events of Daniel's day and the appointed time of the end

together with a specified number of years!

While the first portion of the vision held immediate meaning for Daniel, it more importantly provides very valuable historical data for us. This historical data provides a historical marker from which we can mark the passing of time. The second portion of the vision applies to events that take place during the appointed time of the end.

Immediate meaning

Jesus not only knows and predicts the future, He is also concerned with the present. In Daniel's day, Jesus was deeply grieved with Israel's rebellion and consequently sent them into captivity. Through Jeremiah, Jesus foretold the Babylonian captivity would last 70 years. **"For twenty-three years... the word of the Lord has come to me and I have spoken to you again and again, but you have not listened... Therefore the Lord Almighty says this: 'Because you have not listened to my words, I will summon all the peoples of the north and my servant Nebuchadnezzar, king of Babylon... And I will bring them against this land and its inhabitants and against all the surrounding nations. This whole country will become a desolate wasteland, and these nations will**

serve the king of Babylon seventy years.' " Jeremiah 25:3,8,9,11

Remember, Daniel was one of the Hebrew captives taken into Babylon. He had interpreted the dream concerning the kingdoms of man for Nebuchadnezzar and Daniel knew that another world empire was to follow Babylon. In the vision of Daniel 8, Jesus not only reveals the rise of subsequent empires to Daniel, He even calls them by name! (Jesus even named the Persian general that would overtake the Babylonian empire a hundred years before he was born! See Isaiah 45.) These nations are symbolized as a ram with two horns and a goat with a great horn. These two beasts and their horns represent the kings of the Medo-Persian and Grecian empires respectively.

Daniel also knew that the 70 years of captivity predicted by Jeremiah were about to expire too! He was anxious for his people to be set free to return to Jerusalem. He wondered if the fall of Babylon would bring freedom to his people. The hope of returning to the homeland and the destiny of his people burned deeply within his heart. Daniel wanted to know the outcome of these things so badly that he fasted and prayed for understanding for three weeks! At the end of the fast, Gabriel was sent to Daniel. He had good news and he had bad news.

Babylon's last night

Gabriel told Daniel that the fall of Babylon was imminent. He explained that the ram with two horns represented the kings of Media and Persia that would overthrow Babylon. Daniel was also shown that the Medo-Persian empire would eventually fall. Thus Jesus opened Daniel's mind to a much larger view of His purposes than he understood before.

Gabriel explained to Daniel that God's purpose for Israel was much more inclusive than just returning to Jerusalem. So in the first visit, Gabriel told Daniel about the imminent fall of Babylon. Daniel needed to be prepared - for as it turned out, he would be put on center stage before the Babylonian ruler of the world.

On Babylon's last night, Daniel was awakened by a summons. He was told to immediately appear before Belshazzar, king of Babylon! The king and a thousand of his nobles were having a drunken party when a hand suddenly and mysteriously appeared and wrote something on the wall of the palace. The ominous message was not decipherable to the king, nor his wise men. Eventually, Daniel was called to read the strange message. The old prophet told the king, **"O king, the Most High God gave your father Nebuchadnezzar sovereignty and greatness and glory and splen-**

dor... But when his heart became arrogant and hardened with pride, he was deposed from his throne... until he acknowledged that the Most High God is sovereign over the kingdoms of men... But you his son, O Belshazzar, have not humbled yourself, though you knew all this. Instead, you have set yourself up against the Lord of heaven... You praised the gods of silver and gold, of bronze, iron, wood and stone, which cannot see or hear or understand. But you did not honor the God who holds in his hand your life and all your ways... The meaning is: God has numbered the days of your reign and brought it to an end. You have been weighed on the scales and found wanting. Your kingdom is divided and given to the Medes and Persians." Selections from Daniel 5. The Bible also says that very night Belshazzar was slain and Darius the Mede took over the city of Babylon.

Historical notes

According to history, Babylon fell in the autumn of 538 B.C., as the Medes and Persians came to power. However, both Nebuchadnezzar's and Daniel's visions say the Medes and Persians were not to rule the world forever. They too would pass away. About two centuries later, the defeat of the Persians by Alexander the Great at Arbela in 331 B.C. es-

tablished Greece as a world empire. **Thus history confirms the sequence and chronological portion of the vision concerning the ram and the goat.**

The vision given to Daniel also predicted that the goat (Greece) would become very great, but at the height of his power his large horn was broken off and in its place four prominent horns grew up. At the zenith of world power, Greece's first king, Alexander the Great, died an untimely death at age 32. His kingdom was not passed down to his heirs, but was eventually divided among his four leading generals: Cassander, Lysimachus, Seleucius and Ptolemy. **History again confirms the sequence and chronology of the vision.**

An accurate understanding of Bible prophecy always harmonizes with historical evidence to unveil the foreknowledge of Jesus! Political powers do not come and go by the whim of men. The Apostle Paul said, **"...for there is no authority except that which God has established. The authorities that exist have been established by God."** Romans 13:1

The horn that started small

Remember, Gabriel told Daniel two times that this vision concerns the "appointed time of the end." In future lessons, we shall study the event that marks the time of the end and the horn that starts small. For now, we need to continue with the portion of the vision that relates to Daniel's day so that we may carefully establish some historical dates indicating when the appointed time of the end begins!

During the first year

Some time during the first year of the reign of the Medes and Persians, Daniel was imploring God for the release of the Jews from captivity and the restoration of Jerusalem when Gabriel suddenly appeared before Daniel to continue their discussion on the vision given to Daniel concerning the ram and goat. Daniel says, **"...while I was still in prayer, Gabriel, the man I had seen in the earlier vision, came to me in swift flight about the time of the evening sacrifice."** Daniel 9:21 On this second visit, Gabriel said, **"I have now come to give you insight and understanding... Therefore, consider the message and understand the vision"** (of the 2,300 evenings and mornings). Daniel 9:21-23

(Note: Daniel's concern was focused on the end of the 70 years of Babylonian captivity predicted by Jeremiah. He anticipated the imminent fulfillment of the prophecy. He thought his vision of 2,300 evenings and mornings related to the restoration of Israel and consequently

sought greater understanding. Gabriel returns to talk with Daniel but the subject under discussion is much larger than the restoration of the Jews. In fact, history tells us that Daniel's concern for the freedom of his people was satisfied the year of Gabriel's visit! Captivity ended as prophesied by Jeremiah when Cyrus, king of Persia, released Israel from captivity. The decree was recorded by Ezra. **"In the first year of Cyrus king of Persia, in order to fulfill the word of the Lord spoken by Jeremiah, the Lord moved the heart of Cyrus king of Persia to make a proclamation..."** (freeing Israel). See Ezra 1:1-11.)

So Gabriel returns in this second visit to continue his explanation of the meaning of the vision having 2,300 evenings and mornings. The angel came to Daniel about sundown, the time of the evening sacrifice and said:

1. 70 "sevens" (or weeks) are granted to Israel to:
 a. pay the penalty for their wicked deeds as a nation
 b. put an end to national apostasy
 c. bring in everlasting righteousness
 d. seal up the vision and prophecy
 e. anoint the Most Holy

2. From the issuing of the decree to restore and rebuild Jerusalem, until the Anointed One appears would be 69 weeks.
3. In the middle of the 70th week, the Anointed One would be cut off, also confirm a covenant and He would put an end to sacrifice and offering.
4. Jerusalem and its sanctuary would later be destroyed.
5. Wars and desolations would continue until the end of time.
6. And one who causes desolation will continue until the end of time.

(See Daniel 9:24-27)

Gabriel led Daniel to understand that God's purpose in the future was much larger than Israel returning to Jerusalem. In fact, if you'll compare items 2 and 4 of the prophecy, Gabriel explains that Jerusalem will be rebuilt and afterwards, it will be destroyed again! Daniel was also told that wars would continue until the end of time and the *one* who causes desolation (destructions) would also continue until the end of time.

The angel also told Daniel that the Anointed One (Messiah) would appear 69 weeks after the decree to rebuild Jerusalem. This indicated that yes, Jerusalem would be restored and that the Holy One of Israel would now come. Daniel knew of the promised Messiah for Isaiah had prophesied: "**...The virgin will be with child and will give birth to a son, and will call Him Immanuel... God in the future will honor Galilee of the Gentiles... The people walking in darkness have seen a great light; on those living in the land of the shadow of death a light has dawned... And he will be called Wonderful Counselor, Mighty God, Everlasting Father, Prince of Peace.**" Isaiah 7:14, 9:1,2,6

The most important matter that came out of this visit is that Daniel was led to understand that 70 "sevens" were being placed upon the Jews for several reasons. The ultimate purpose (see item 1 above) was to prepare a people to receive Messiah!

An appointment with Messiah

Review the six elements of Gabriel's talk with Daniel. You will notice that the message given to Daniel clearly states that from the decree to restore and rebuild Jerusalem until Messiah appears would be 69 weeks.

God's timing is always perfect. Three keys unlock this important message from Gabriel allowing us to see the beauty of His timing. We will look at the first two keys in this study:

KEY I - A day for a year

The words "70 sevens" refer to an understanding the Jews had regarding time. A "seven" was a time period of seven years. Seven "sevens" (or 49 years) was a revolving time period called a "Jubilee." According to Leviticus 25 & 26, the Jews were to count years by sevens for the land was to have a rest every 7th year. Israel was not to sow or plant their fields in the 7th year. God promised to make their fields so fruitful during the sixth year that work in fields during the 7th year would be unnecessary!

Even more, after the year of rest at the 49th year, (the 7th sabbatical,) the year of Jubilee occurred! The year of Jubilee was the 50th year which was also the first year of the next "seven." During the Jubilee year, land that had been sold was returned to the family. Debts were cancelled and real estate was returned to the original owner! The "seven" and the Jubilee were a lesson designed by Jesus to teach Israel that one day, He would both redeem (buy back) those faithful and obedient to the Lord and would return them to their original homeland - the garden of Eden. The great debt of sin would be paid in full for those willing to live by faith!

Daniel understood that 70 "sevens" of years meant 490 years or 10 Jubilees. This time period of grace would be granted to Israel as a final effort to fulfill God's plan for them as a nation. Daniel must have sorrowed to hear that Jerusalem would be rebuilt and then destroyed again. Would his people be prepared to accept the Messiah?

Daniel was told the Anointed One (the Messiah) would appear 483 years (69 x 7 = 483) after the decree to restore and rebuild Jerusalem. Although three decrees were given on behalf of Israel, the decree granting the necessary money, governmental power and freedom of worship was given by Artaxerxes in the 7th year of his reign. The decree is recorded in Ezra 7 and was issued in the fall of 457 B.C.

Note: Some challenge the use of the decree dated 457 B.C. since there were actually three decrees. Fortunately, enough historical evidence is available to show the particular decree, issued in 457 B.C., is the one that fulfills the prophecy.

If our understanding and application of the 69 "sevens" is correct, Jesus, the Messiah, the Anointed One, should appear 483 years after the decree to restore and rebuild Jerusalem. Did He appear before the Jewish people that year?

"In the fifteenth year of the reign of Tiberius Caesar - when Pontius Pilate was governor of Judea, Herod tetrarch of Galilee... The people were waiting expectantly and were all wondering in their hearts if John (the Baptist) might

possibly be the Christ.... When all the people were being baptized, Jesus was baptized too... Jesus ...was about thirty years old when be began his ministry." Selections from Luke 3.

From historical sources we can calculate the fifteenth year of Tiberius Caesar that Luke speaks of. It is 27 A.D. which is exactly 483 years from the decree in 457 B.C. by Artaxerxes! Jesus, who set the time of His appearing - appeared right on time.

KEY II - Jesus dies on time

Gabriel said that in the middle of the 70th "seven" the Anointed One would be cut off (literally cut down), that He would also confirm a covenant and He would put an end to sacrifice and offering.

Since a "seven" represents 7 years, the 70th week of this prophecy is 7 years long. The 70th week began with 27 A.D. and reaches to 34 A.D. The middle mark (or middle of the week) between these years is 31 A.D. Several points converge during this year:

1. Jesus was crucified in the spring of the year during the Passover feast which was celebrated in the Spring. John 19:14

2. It appears that Passover fell on Saturday that year. John 19:31 (Note: Some scholars believe the accompanying eclipse of the sun at Jesus' death is recorded as being Friday, March 25, 31 A.D.)

3. Gabriel indicated that Messiah was to be "cut off" (literally translated: cut down). Was He cut down by his own people? Stephen, the first Christian martyr cried out to the Sanhedrin regarding the crucifixion of Jesus **"...you have betrayed and murdered him!"** Acts 7:52

4. Did Messiah put an end to sacrifices and offerings? Paul says, **"God ...cancelled the written code, with its regulations, that was against us and that stood opposed to us; he took it away, nailing it to the cross."** Colossians 2:13,14

5. Did Jesus confirm the covenant? Again, Paul says, **"This salvation, which was first announced by the Lord, was confirmed to us by those who heard him."** Hebrews 2:3

History agrees

According to the prophecy, Jesus died *exactly on time*. As the High Priest was about to slay the Passover lamb in Jerusalem's temple, out on Golgotha's hill - Jesus, the Passover Lamb of God died for the sins of the whole world.

An angel immediately flew to the temple and tore open the heavy temple veil from top to bottom that separated the Holy place from the Most Holy place. This act signified the end of the sacrificial system. Jesus had confirmed His covenant with His own blood. The religious services which had been required of Israel were now unnecessary. The penalty of sin which they had pointed to was now paid in full. The shadow of earthly things disappeared in the fulfillment of Christ's death. The ceremonies were nailed to the cross.

(Note: When the veil was torn open, the great multitude that gathered for the passover beheld the contents of the Most Holy place of the temple for the first time. The room's sole property was darkness. The ark of the covenant which had been hidden by Jeremiah at the time of the Babylonian captivity was never found and remains hidden to this very day! How symbolic that darkness not only filled the inner place of Israel's religious shrine, great darkness filled the hearts of the worshipers too.)

Summary

1. In 27 A.D., the fifteenth year of Tiberius Caesar, the Jews *anticipated* the appearing of Messiah. Luke 3:15 Even the Samaritans hoped for the coming Messiah. The woman at the well said: **"...I know that Messiah is coming... when he comes, he will explain everything to us."** John 4:25 Mathematically, 27 A.D. is the 483rd year from the decree given by Artaxerxes in 457 B.C.

2. Jesus was baptized in 27 A.D., being 30 years of age. A man had to reach this age before he could serve as a priest. See Numbers 4:3.

3. "Elijah" as promised in Malachi 4:5 preceded the year 27 A.D. He came in the person of John the Baptist to prepare the "way of the Lord." See Matthew 11:14.

4. Jesus, who gave this vision to Daniel 550 years before He was born, understood the timing and fulfillment of the prophecy, for He said at the beginning of His ministry on earth, **"The time has come...."** Mark 1:14,15 Again, Jesus speaking after His baptism in Nazareth said, **"The Spirit of the Lord is on me... to proclaim the** *year* **of the Lord's favor."** Luke 4:18,19

5. Christ died precisely on time. Jesus, The Passover Lamb of God, died on the *very day* the ceremonial service had pointed forward to for centuries. 31 A.D. is also historically confirmed by the Council of Caesarea in 196 A.D., the Alexandrian Chronicle, and

early historians Maximus Monachus, and Cedrenus.

6. Each time the story is told of the birth of Jesus, the story of the wise men is told. What many people don't know is that the wise men were students of prophecy. They came from the East (area around Babylon) where they had found and studied Daniel's writings. By understanding that a priest in Israel had to be 30 years of age before beginning his ministry, they calculated the end of the 483 years and then subtracted 30 years from their conclusion to determine the year of Jesus' birth. When you consider the fact that their roundtrip journey took about 2 years, you can begin to appreciate the intensity of their desire to attend the birth of Messiah. Wise men do not go to such lengths on a whim. Like the prophets Simeon and Anna, they longed to "personally" behold the Saviour of the world. Their presence at the birth of Jesus also confirms the accuracy of this prophecy for there are no other prophecies in the Bible pinpointing the time of Messiah's appearing other than this one found in Daniel 9.

The fullness of time

Paul succinctly sums up Daniel's prophecy by saying, **"But when the time had fully come, God sent his Son..."** (Galatians 4:4). Can any question remain that God's timing is less than perfect?

In our next study, the third key will be explained. It holds a special message for Christians!

Quiz

1. What were the two kingdoms to follow Babylon?

2. The vision of Daniel has two parts. Why is the first part important?

3. Prophecy is _____ in advance. History is _____ fulfilled.

4. What two prophetic keys help us understand the appearing of Messiah?

5. Bonus: How did the wise men know the timing of Messiah's birth?

What time is it?

Part II

Lesson 8

Review

In our last lesson we began looking into Daniel's prophecy concerning the appointed time of the end. Even though the prophecy spans several centuries, it's primary focus is the appointed time of the end.

The prophecy actually contains two parts. The first part held immediate meaning for Daniel and as we shall see, it also establishes a valuable historical footing or marker so that we might know when the end of time arrives. So far, we have discussed 3 dates. These were 457 B.C., 27 and 31 A.D. The correctness of 457 B.C. is marked by the decree of Artaxerxes (Ezra 7) to restore and rebuild Jerusalem. This date is wonderfully confirmed by Jesus beginning His ministry precisely on time 483 years later - during the 15th year of Tiberius Caesar.

The 15th year of Tiberius Caesar is 27 A.D. Further, Jesus, the Passover Lamb, died right on time three and a half years later at the Passover feast in the Spring of 31 A.D.

Three keys help us unlock the vision of Daniel's prophecy. The first key requires an understanding of the time period known as a "seven." A "seven" represents 7 years. (See Leviticus 26.) Every seven years, the Jews did not plant crops for this year was a rest or sabbatical. Thus 70 "sevens" represent 490 literal years. The appearing of Messiah 483 years later (69 "sevens") confirms the correctness of this interpretation.

The second key is the historical timing of Christ's death as it relates to the prophecy. Jesus died precisely on time in the middle of the 70th week which is 31 A.D. Some students of prophecy believe the 70th week is broken into two parts. In this view, the 70th week contains a time period of 3.5 years, a gap of many centuries, then the final time period of 3.5 years. If this is true, the *middle* of the 70th week cannot be determined! For example, we can only compute the middle of the 70th week when we know the beginning and ending dates. The middle year between 27 A.D. and 34 A.D. is 31 A.D. However, if the 70th week is not 7 consecutive years, the middle of the 70th week cannot be determined until the end of the week is known.

Other students of prophecy attempt to move the entire 70th week of seven years to the end of time. If this is done, the birth, death and resurrection of Jesus are completely missed! Further, those moving the 70th week of seven years to the end of time disconnect the 69 weeks from the 70th week. If this is done, no historical marker pinpoints the beginning of the seven years of the 70th week.

The 70 weeks of 490 years must stand together as one unit of time. These years were allotted to the Jewish nation to accomplish certain things which Gabriel explained to Daniel. Jesus Himself confirmed the beginning of the 70th week of seven years by beginning His ministry in 27 A.D. and by confirming the covenant by His death three and a half years later in 31 A.D.

The third and last key that unlocks this portion of the prophecy relates to the end of the 70th week - 34 A.D. At this point in time, the destiny of the Jewish nation was decided.

KEY III - The destiny of the Jews

Let us review Gabriel's comments to Daniel concerning the Jews:

"70 sevens (or weeks) are granted to Israel to":

  a. pay the penalty for their wicked deeds as a nation
  b. put an end to national apostasy
  c. bring in everlasting righteousness
  d. seal up the vision and prophecy
  e. anoint the Most Holy

The first two elements of the prophecy above relate to Jewish behavior and the last three elements relate to promised glory. The Jews knew they were special to God. They knew that Messiah would come through their bloodline. This prophecy underscores the special relationship between Jesus and His people. If they would turn to Jesus, Israel could still fulfill His purpose. They would have the opportunity to anoint the Most Holy One of Israel! They would have the opportunity to bring in everlasting righteousness. Just think, if the Jews had taken advantage of the promises given, the history of the world would be far different than it has been! If the Jews had fulfilled their calling, they could have "sealed up the vision and prophecy" so that the destruction also contained in this prophecy would not take place!

This prophecy (and a few others in the Bible) contains a conditional element. If Israel did not meet the conditions set forth, Jerusalem would again be destroyed and wars and desolations would continue to the end of the world. Even more, the "one" who causes wars and desolations would be free to continue his work until the end.

This prophecy illuminates a very serious and important point. When Jesus chose Israel to be a special people to Himself, He wanted them to clearly understand that the relationship depended upon certain conditions. Jesus told the Jews through Moses, **"...If you do not obey the Lord your God and do not carefully follow all his commands and decrees I am giving you today, all these curses will come upon you and overtake you... The Lord will send on you curses, confusion and rebuke in everything you put your hand to, until you are destroyed and come to sudden ruin because of the evil you have done in forsaking him."** Deuteronomy 28:15,20

So, seventy "sevens" or 490 years of probationary time was granted to Israel. It was their last opportunity for reconciliation with Jesus. God had suffered with their stiff-necks and hard hearts for about 1300 years, and this was their final opportunity. If they did not respond to the offer, Jesus would do something else. Several important factors supplement this portion of the prophecy.

During the 70 "sevens" Israel was to atone for their wicked ways as a nation by experiencing revival and reformation. Repentance means the forsaking of sin! During this probationary time of 490 years (457 B.C. to 34 A.D.), the Jewish nation was to "bring in everlasting righteousness" by forsaking sin and measuring up to the high standards set forth by Jesus.

70 "sevens" - a measure of forgiveness

The Jewish people knew the 70 sevens were probationary. They knew national apostasy brought on the Babylonian captivity. They knew they were given a last chance. In fact, Jesus used the 70 "sevens" mentioned in Daniel 9 as an expression of forbearance when Peter asked, **"...Lord, how many times shall I forgive my brother when he sins against me? Up to seven times? Jesus answered, I tell you, not seven times, but seventy times seven."** Matthew 18:21,22

The Jews were to bring in everlasting righteousness. What does "bringing in everlasting righteousness" mean? It means that Jesus wanted the nation to operate on principles of righteousness. This can only happen if the people of the nation love righteousness! Jesus wanted a people that loved the Lord with all their hearts and their neighbors as themselves! The Jews clearly knew that their favored status with God was conditional. Moses had said, **"If you fully obey the Lord your God and carefully follow all his commands... blessings will come... However, if you do not obey the Lord your God and do not carefully follow all his commands... curses will come upon you..."** (Deuteronomy 28).

The last year of the 70th "seven" occurred in 34 A.D. This year is very important for it represents the last year of Jewish probation as a nation to receive and fulfill God's promises. As the 490 years of probationary time expired, so did Israel's last opportunity to fulfill God's glorious plan for them as a nation. Like Sodom and Gomorrah, Jericho and the wicked nations of Canaan, Israel passed the point of divine forbearance. They had been forgiven "seventy times seven." The Jewish nation like the heathen nations before them, came to the end of divine mercy and Jesus dealt with them accordingly. Jesus had clearly warned Israel of His actions on the heathen and made it clear He would do the same to them saying, **"...so I punished (the land of Canaan) for its sin and the land vomited out its inhabitants... And if you defile the land, it will vomit you out as it vomited out the nations that were before you."** Leviticus 18:25,28

Israel abandoned

A series of events transpired in 34 A.D. that shows Jesus terminated His relationship with the nation of Israel. Before looking at them, let's review Israel's relation to Jesus:

- The Jews rejected Jesus as the Messiah, the Saviour of the world. They could not see beyond the shadows of ceremonies and services. For salvation, they preferred the blood of animals to faith in the blood of Jesus.

- The Jews failed to bring in national repentance; thus their corporate rebellion led them to crucify Jesus and persecute those who represented His work on earth. Their religious pride blinded them in their transgressions.

- Jesus, knowing He would die in 31 A.D. when He gave the prophecy to Daniel, did not base the close of Jewish probation on

His death. For three and a half years *after* His death, His disciples pressed upon the leaders in Jerusalem the prophecies concerning the resurrected Messiah! Oh, what divine mercy, what divine patience and forbearance! Jesus, before his death predicted the Jews would reject the gospel, saying, **"If they do not listen to Moses and the Prophets, they will not be convinced even if someone rises from the dead."** Luke 16:31

The straw that breaks the camel's back

The most significant historical event recorded in the Bible during the last year of probationary time (34 A.D.) was the stoning of the Christian deacon, Stephen. The Sanhedrin (the Jewish supreme court) sentenced Stephen to death for preaching, "Jesus risen from the dead." The killing of Stephen initiated a calculated and open persecution of all Christians by the Jews (see Acts 7).

Jesus chooses others to carry His gospel

What did Jesus do from heaven in 34 A.D. in response to the decision of the Jews?

1.   Jesus gave Peter a vision about unclean animals. While in vision, Peter thought the command to "kill and eat" the unclean animals had dietary implications. Peter said, **"I have never eaten anything impure or unclean."** Acts 10:14 But a voice from heaven said, **"...do not call anything impure that God has made clean."** Acts 10:15 Three times this happened. Peter wondered about the vision. What did it mean? While thinking about the meaning, the Holy Spirit said, **"...Simon, three men are looking for you. So get up and go downstairs. Do not hesitate to go with them, for I have sent them."** Acts 10:19,20

The apostle Peter was invited to the home of a Roman centurion, Cornelius. Cornelius was a Gentile and as such, was regarded as "unclean" by the Jews. But Cornelius wanted to hear the gospel. He was a God-fearing man.

Peter was very perplexed about going into the home of a Gentile (which was unlawful for a Jew to enter), but the Holy Spirit had said, "Go!" Upon arriving at the home of Cornelius, Peter said, **"...you are well aware that it is against our law for a Jew to associate with a Gentile or visit him. But God has shown me that I should not call any man** impure or unclean. **So when I was sent for, I came without raising any objection. May I ask why you sent for me?"** Acts 10:28,29 Peter now understood the meaning of the vision. A great change was taking place. He dimly began to see that the commission of representing God on earth belonged to the Christians - instead of the Jews. (Compare Acts 10, Matthew 28)

2.   Perhaps the strongest response of Jesus to Israel's final rejection in 34 A.D. was to take one of Israel's brightest and best and "make" a Christian out of him. The conversion of Saul to the apostle Paul and his life of service is a story only excelled by the life of Jesus. Saul, the Jewish persecutor, became Paul, the persecuted Christian, an apostle sent specifically to the Gentiles. Jesus told Ananias concerning Saul, **"...This man is my chosen instrument to carry my name before the Gentiles and their kings and before the people of Israel. I will show him how much he must suffer for my name."** Acts 9:15,16

At the expiration of the 70 "sevens" in 34 A.D., Israel had failed to meet the conditions of the prophecy.

Therefore, Jesus raised up a new group of "chosen" people called "Christians." Jesus set out to accomplish through the Christian Church what the Jews had failed to do. He gave the Christian Church a renewed covenant, a renewed faith, a renewed understanding of His character and most of all, a theology based on His life, death, resurrection and priestly ministry.

Three keys confirm historical footing

The three keys now work together to unlock the longest time prophecy in the Bible. Note that 457 B.C. is now historically confirmed with three dates. First, Jesus began His ministry on time (27 A.D.), He died on time (31 A.D.), and Israel lost favored status at the end of the seventy "sevens" (34 A.D.). The promised destruction of the city and the temple also mentioned in the prophecy (Daniel 9:26) occurred in 70 A.D. Rome completely destroyed Jerusalem in that seige. What a sad ending to such a glorious beginning.

The appointed time of the end

The vision of Daniel is comprehensive. As you can see, the Bible is a storehouse of treasures and those who study prophecy study the deep things of God.

Now that the accuracy of 457 B.C. has been "nailed" down, we can understand another portion of Daniel's vision. Remember, Daniel heard two angels talking in the first segment of his vision. One angel asked a very complex question that really contains five questions. They were:

a. How long will it take for the vision to be fulfilled?
b. How will the daily be taken away?
c. How long will the rebellion that causes desolation last?
d. How long will the sanctuary be surrendered?
e. How long will the saints be trampled upon?

The answers to these five questions are sprinkled throughout this comprehensive prophecy. To appreciate the answers to all these questions, the student must understand Revelation's story too. For now, we will look at the fourth question, **"How long will the sanctuary be surrendered?."**

Daniel heard an immediate answer to this question. One angel said, **"...it will take 2,300 evenings and mornings; then the sanctuary will be reconsecrated"** (Daniel 8:14). Daniel heard the answer, but didn't understand the meaning. Gabriel said, **"The vision of the (2,300) evenings and mornings that has been given you is true, but seal up the vision, for it concerns the distant future. I, Daniel, was exhausted and lay ill for several days. Then I got up and went about the king's business. I was appalled by the vision; it was beyond understanding"** Daniel 8:26,27

A year passes

Daniel meditated on the vision from time to time. As any student of prophecy, he carefully studied all that had been revealed through past prophets for understanding on God's purposes and plans. He wanted to know the meaning of what he had seen. One day, while Daniel was in earnest prayer, Gabriel came to give more information about the vision.

(Note: The reason we have spent considerable effort establishing the historical importance and accuracy of 457 B.C. is because this date also marks the beginning of the 2,300 evenings and mornings!)

Seventy "sevens" are cut off

Remember, Gabriel told Daniel, **"Seventy sevens are decreed for your people..."** Daniel 9:24 The Hebrew word translated "decreed" is chathak (see Strong's Hebrew and Chaldee dictionary #2852) which literally means, "cut off." What Gabriel told Daniel is that the seventy "sevens" are "cut off" from the vision of the 2,300 mornings and evenings. In other words, the 490 years are a subset or part of the larger vision.

The relationship between the vision recorded in Daniel 8 and the comments of Gabriel in Daniel 9 is clearly established for Daniel identifies Gabriel as the one he had talked with in the earlier segment of this vision. (Daniel 9:21) Even though Daniel desired to know the meaning of the vision concerning the 2,300 evenings and mornings, Gabriel does not directly address the first segment of Daniel's vision except to say the seventy sevens are cut off from the longer time period.

What does the scripture mean? **"...it will take 2,300 evenings and mornings; then the sanctuary will be reconsecrated."** Daniel 8:14 Several elements have to be addressed to explain the meaning of this verse.

1. Since creation, an evening and a morning represents one day. **"God called the light 'day'**

and the darkness he called 'night'. And there was evening, and there was morning the first day." Genesis 1:5 In Bible times a day began at evening (twilight). This was followed by midnight, morning and noon. A 24-hour day lasted from evening to evening.

2. 2,300 evenings and mornings means 2,300 days. Since the seventy "sevens" (490 years) are "cut off" from this prophecy, we know that this prophecy represents one day as one year. Here's how: the seventy "sevens" are a subset of the larger time prophecy, consequently, they are "cut off" or cut out of the larger time prophecy. If the seventy "sevens" use the day for a year process, then 2,300 days have to follow the day/year structure too!

3. If we proceed 2,300 years from 457 B.C. we arrive at 1844.

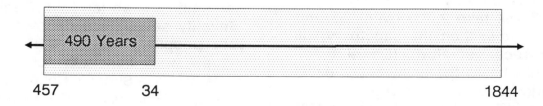

490 Years are a subset of the 2300 Years

2300

- 457

1843

From mathematics alone, we note the date would be 1843. This is because math uses a number scale that includes a zero. Notice the following scale:

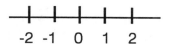

-2 -1 0 1 2

You will notice that 2 years (or two spaces) exist between -1 and 1 for this scale moves from -1 to 0 to 1. When the dating of time relative to Christ's birth was put together, the 0 year was left out. It is not possible to say 0 B.C. or 0 A.D. So any periods of time that span B.C. to A.D. must have an additional year added to be mathematically correct. So 1843 +1 equals 1844.

4.   What does the Bible mean when it says that the sanctuary will be reconsecrated or cleansed after 2,300 evenings and mornings?

Some Christians believe that the Jews are still God's chosen people and that Israel has an important part for the cause of Jesus at the end of the world. Thirty-eight hundred years of Jewish history and tradition indicates the Jewish nation will never accept Jesus Christ as the promised Messiah. (Yes, a few Jews have come to accept Jesus as their personal Messiah, but as a nation, they haven't changed.)

It is true that Israel plays a part in the end of the world - but it is not a glorious part. This prophecy of Daniel predicts that Israel (and most of the world) will accept the great imposter that is coming upon the earth claiming to be God! More will be said about this when we study Revelation 9.

The sanctuary to which the vision relates exists in heaven, where Jesus serves as our High Priest. Remember, this vision primarily applies to the "appointed time of the end." The rebuilt sanctuary of the Jews was destroyed in 70 A.D. by the Romans because the privilege of being God's chosen nation was forfeited by the end of the 70th week (34 A.D.). Thus Jesus prophesied to the Pharisees, **"Look, your house (temple) is left to you desolate."** Matthew 23:38

Remember, the Apostle Paul confirms the presence of the heavenly sanctuary, **"...we do have such a high priest, who sat down at the right hand of the throne of the Majesty in heaven, and who** serves in the sanctuary, the true tabernacle set up by the Lord, not by man."   Hebrews 8:1,2

So, the vision of the 2,300 days is connected to the services of the heavenly sanctuary that is to be restored or reconsecrated!   How can this be?

The sanctuary restored

The Christian faith is built upon the achievement of Jesus. He came to earth, was tempted beyond anything humans will ever face, yet lived a sinless life and willingly died at the hands of His own people to pay the penalty of sin. He returned to heaven and sat down at the right hand of the Father to intercede through the merits of His blood for the human race. Christ's work in heaven from His ascension to 1844 may be thought of as that of a priest in the earthly sanctuary.

Since the Old Testament sanctuary built in the wilderness was a representation of the one in heaven, services there represent or "shadow" processes of services actually taking place in heaven! Paul clearly understood this point. Talking about the role of priests, he says, **"They serve at a sanctuary that is copy and shadow of what is in heaven. This is why Moses was warned when he was about to build the tabernacle: 'See to it that you make everything according to the pattern shown you on the mountain.'"**   Hebrews 8:5

Since the Jews failed to respond to the probationary time period of the seventy "sevens," the *intended* purpose of the rebuilt temple and restored services were never fulfilled. Consequently, Jesus said, "Your temple is left desolate." Here is a profound point: What Jesus intended to do in the earthly temple would have to be done in the heavenly one!

In a later lesson, we will learn that Jesus was coronated as High Priest in 1844 in heaven and began a very special work. It is His coronation and work as our High Priest that reconsecrates or restores the sanctuary process! This is not to say that Jesus wasn't busy with heavenly business from His ascension in 31 A.D. to 1844. No! Jesus was very intimately involved with the development of the Christian Church. Jesus showed Daniel that certain matters would develop during the "times of the Gentiles." Some of these prophetic matters are very fascinating and will be looked at in our next lesson.

The point is made that Jesus clearly placed a long span of time between Daniel's day and the "appointed time of the end" - 2,300 years to be exact! Since Jesus personally confirmed the accuracy of 457 B.C. with his baptism and death, 1844 is just as certain too! We shall soon see that

1844 marks the beginning of the end.

Summary

Daniel 8 and 9 are inseparably linked together to show us when the "appointed time of the end" arrives chronologically. The accuracy of 1844 is as certain as the beginning date of 457 B.C., the baptism of Jesus in 27 A.D., the death of Jesus in 31 A.D. and the gospel given to the Gentiles in 34 A.D. Three keys unlock the meaning of the seventy "sevens" and the resulting harmony is both scriptural and historical.

Isn't it interesting that what the Jews forfeited, the Christians inherited? In our next study, we will look into prophetic events that take place between the ascension of Jesus and 1844. We will see how history repeats itself!

Quiz

1.   The Jews understood that a "seven" represented ____ years.

2.   How many years existed between the decree to restore and rebuild Jerusalem and the appearing of Messiah?

3.   Jesus died in the middle of the _____ week.

4.   Peter first thought the vision of unclean animals related to diet, then understood that the vision related to:

5.   Seventy "sevens" were cut off of what?

Notes:

Notes:

What time is it?

Part III

Lesson 9

Thus far we've studied the prophetic mechanism that reaches 1844 chronologically. Why is 1844 so important? What does the Bible mean when it says, "then shall the sanctuary be restored"? The answer to this question is not complicated when the underlying issues involved are properly understood.

Even though the prophetic importance of 1844 is not appreciated by many people at this time, this is about to change! Interest in this subject will rise from obscurity to intense interest in the near future. As we will see, God has ordained that earth shall know that "the appointed time of the end has come!" For the sake of review, notice that the longest time prophecy in the Bible is built solidly upon four historical moments confirmed in scripture:

1. The decree to restore and rebuild Jerusalem occurred in 457 B.C. Ezra 7
2. 69 weeks later (483 years) Jesus was baptized and anointed by the Holy Spirit in 27 A.D. Luke 3
3. Jesus was crucified in 31 A.D. at the time of the Passover feast - right on time. John 19
4. Probationary time for the Jews as a nation ended in 34 A.D. when the privilege of representing God was transferred to the Christians. Acts 7-10

According to Daniel 8:14, the cleansing of the heavenly sanctuary began in 1844. The cleansing or restoration of the heavenly sanctuary is very similar to the ancient Day of Atonement service conducted in the wilderness sanctuary. What should this mean to us right now?

Two failures

To appreciate the importance of 1844, we look back to the 70 weeks of probationary time given to the Jewish nation. The 490 years must be contrasted with 1800 years of failed opportunities. Note the diagram below:

ultimately crucified the One who chose them. The promised curses have come to pass. Israel was abandoned by Jesus as His chosen people in 34 A.D. - it was their choice.

So, Jesus chose twelve disciples to displace the twelve tribes. If Israel

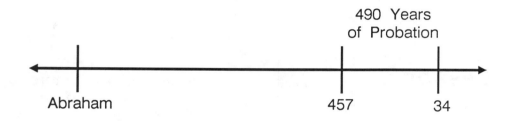

1800 years allotted to the Jews

The "appointed time of the end" follows a similar parallel. 1844 marks the *beginning* of the appointed time of the end (just as 457 B.C. marked the beginning of the 490 years) and the second coming marks the *end* of the appointed time of the end (just as 34 A.D. marked the end of Jewish probation). The 490 years granted to Israel and the appointed time of the end serve a similar function in that the appointed time of the end is earth's last time period for the Gentiles!

Remember, Jesus chose Israel to be a special people. He patiently dealt with them as a nation for approximately 1800 years. They rejected His love and affection, and

would be stiff-necked and rebellious, He would have to start over. He formed a new group of people called "Christians." These were to accomplish what the Jews had failed to do. These were to represent His character and love before the world. These were to be channels through which His blessings of love could flow. These were sent out to the Gentiles of the world. The Gentiles were to have their day of opportunity! Jesus told his disciples, **"They (the Jews) will fall by the sword and will be taken as prisoners to all the nations. Jerusalem will be trampled on by the Gentiles until the times (years)** of the Gentiles are fulfilled." Luke 21:24

The times (or years of probation) of the Gentiles is not over yet! We will see in Revelation that Jesus intends that every Gentile hear the gospel call. So, turning from the Jews, Jesus gave the gospel commission to the Christian Church. Maybe they would fulfill their opportunity. But history confirms that the Church also failed to do what Jesus wanted them to do! Here, in brief, is the story.

Jesus starts over

For three and one half years Jesus patiently taught the disciples about His kingdom of love. After His ascension, the disciples, endowed with the power of the Holy Spirit, labored for Jesus just as He commanded, **"Therefore go and make disciples of all nations, baptizing them in the name of the Father and of the Son and of the Holy Spirit, and teaching them to obey everything I have commanded you... "** Matthew 28:19,20

Satan wasted no time in opposing the developing work of Jesus on earth. His desire for the destruction of Christians was as fierce and determined as it was against the Jews. Satan used every evil resource at his disposal to destroy the knowledge and love of God be-

stowed upon the Christian church. How did he do it?

Satan wages war

Satan began with torture and death. Those first Christians were defenseless against the rage of "that old serpent, the devil" and for the first three centuries of the church's history, Christians were relentlessly persecuted by both Jews and Romans. Ironically, persecution of the church accomplished what the Romans and Jews wanted least. As Christians scattered for their lives, they carried the gospel of Jesus with them throughout the world!

But after while, Satan saw that the more he persecuted the church, the larger and more dedicated it became. Persecution served to keep the church pure and its doctrines free of human sophistry. This was not the desired effect, so Satan launched a new form of warfare against the church. He applied the adage, "If you can't lick 'em, join 'em." Satan joined the church! Where he had failed in destroying the truth through persecution he would succeed by leading the church to corrupt the teachings of Jesus. He corrupted the truth through educated and eloquent men in leadership positions. While these men outwardly claimed to be disciples of Christ they were far less than "born again."

Daniel predicted the Christian Church would become antichrist centuries before it existed!

The prophecy recorded in Daniel 7 clearly identifies the corrupting influence of Satan upon the Christian Church and its destructive effects upon God's people. A few comments are presented on this amazing prophecy.

Remember king Nebuchadnezzar's dream? He saw the kingdoms of man outlined in the form of a man made of various metals. A few years after the king's vision, Daniel had a vision that essentially covered the same kingdoms and time periods. The prophetic process of repetition and enlargement is clearly seen here. The king saw a broad picture of future events and Daniel saw the same thing but with more detail!

Daniel sees a lion, bear, leopard and a terrible beast

This vision is recorded in Daniel 7. You should read this entire chapter from your Bible to understand all that Daniel saw. Basically, Daniel's dream contained four strange beasts. They were unusual beasts in that features were added to their bodies to highlight certain characteristics. They were:

1. A lion with eagle wings
2. A bear with three ribs in its mouth
3. A leopard with four wings and four heads
4. A terrible beast with ten horns

Daniel was particularly awed at the fourth beast having ten horns because it had unusual power, was indescribable in its fury, and ultimately focused its wrath on the saints of God.

The accompanying angel told Daniel the four beasts represented four kingdoms that would rise from the earth. Many historians agree that the four beasts seen by Daniel represent the *same kingdoms* seen by Nebuchadnezzar. The Bible often parallels prophetic themes with additional information to help us understand the meaning of a prophecy. (Compare the beasts with Lesson 6, page 9.) So, the lion represented Babylon; the bear, Medo-Persia; the leopard, Grecia and the fourth beast represents the fourth kingdom, Rome. The harmony of the chronological sequence and the contents of the visions with historical confirmation places this matter beyond reasonable controversy.

The fourth beast

Even though Daniel observed four beasts in his vision, he was most distressed and awed by the fourth beast, for it was very different than the other beasts. This beast persecuted the saints. The following is a brief summary of the fourth beast as described in Daniel 7 and the little horn that came out of the fourth beast:

1. It starts out as the fourth world empire.
2. It is unusual in strength and furious with enemies.
3. It has teeth of iron.
4. Out of this kingdom ten horns (or kings) arise.
5. After the ten kings appear, a little horn arises and, in so doing, uproots three of the original ten kings.
6. This new horn has all the fierce qualities of its parent, the terrible fourth beast.
7. The little horn power becomes a great horn - much stronger than any of the remaining seven horns.
8. The little horn power blasphemes the God of Heaven.
9. The little horn power wars against the saints for a specified time.
10. The little horn power "thinks" to change times and laws.
11. The little horn power endures until the end of the world.

Historically, the fourth beast has been clearly identified as Rome for almost 1500 years. The little horn power (items 5-11 above) has likewise been identified by students of prophecy for almost fifteen centuries as an antichrist power. There is no question concerning the character of the little horn. It is antichrist. The identity of this antichrist power is necessary because it has a leading role in last day events!

The little horn power is the great spiritual power that came out of the fourth kingdom, i.e., Rome! For more than seven hundred years students of prophecy have called the little horn power the universal Christian Church or the Roman Catholic Church.

Note: The following is a brief description of what happened in the course of history to the Christian Church as it moved farther and farther away from the truth of God's Word by replacing the teachings of the Bible with man-made traditions or doctrines. The sponsors of this seminar sincerely believe there are many wonderful and dedicated Christian people within the Roman Catholic Church who love their church and faithfully practice its teachings. Many of its members have not had an opportunity or sufficient reason to consider the Protestant view of the Church's history. Even further, many Catholics have little or no knowledge concerning the origins of its doctrines or teachings. Upon examination, many

Catholics are shocked to learn that many Church doctrines have no Biblical basis whatsoever.

Process of identification

By what means did the Protestant Reformers identify the Catholic Church as being antichrist? A collection of writings calling for reformation within the Roman Church began to circulate about 1300 A.D. As time passed, the number of people calling for change significantly increased. Those denouncing teachings or doctrines promoted by the Church that had no biblical basis became known as "protestors" or "protestants." Their united plea was simple, "Away with the harsh and unjust rule of Roman clerics teaching man-made traditions. Give us the Bible alone as the Word of God. *Sola Scriptura!*"

The pleas of the protestors provoked powerful church officials so that eventually, any or all protestors were condemned to the dungeon, stake or sword. Persecution, torture, discouragement and death are some of Satan's most persuasive tools!

Some of the better known reformers involved in the initial call for reformation were Wycliff, Huss, Jerome, Luther, Calvin, Knox, and Tyndale. As the conflict between the Protestants and the Catholic Church grew, educated men throughout Europe began identifying the little horn power in Daniel 7 as the Papacy. Their conclusions were generally derived by the following steps:

Rome - fourth beast

The terrible fourth beast in Daniel 7 is historically confirmed and recognized as civil Rome, the fourth universal kingdom of the world. Civil Rome came to power about 168 B.C. with the overthrow of Greece. The powerful teeth of iron belonging to the terrible beast (remember, the legs of Nebuchadnezzar's image representing this fourth kingdom in Daniel 2 were also made of iron) fittingly described the unusual strength of Rome's military legions since they were first to extensively use iron weapons.

Ten horns overtake Rome

The ten horns which overcame Rome were recognized by reformers as the ten kingdoms into which civil Rome (Europe) was divided around 476 A.D. They were: Ostrogoths, Heruli, Franks, Vandals, Lombards, Visigoths, Suevi, Burgundians, Alamanni and the Anglo-Saxons.

Little horn overtakes three horns

According to Daniel, the little horn power was to become prominent after the ten horns were active. While it may be said the Christian

Church began at the time of Christ, it must be understood that the church grew from infancy to great political power over a period of about five centuries. According to Daniel's prophecy, the little horn power would become stronger than any of the ten kingdoms represented by the ten horns! A major point is made that *after* the ten horns are in power, *then* the little horn rises to power.

According to the prophecy, the little horn would distinguish itself from the other kingdoms, by "plucking" up three of the original ten horns or kingdoms by their roots. The Roman Church (the little horn) plucked up three horns (i.e., three tribal nations) known as the Ostrogoths, Vandals, and Heruli as it rose to power. These three tribal nations were destroyed over a theological dispute on the deity of Christ. Historically, this dispute is known as the "Arian controversy." The dominating influence of the emerging Christian Church upon the remaining seven tribal nations is clearly demonstrated in this portion of the prophecy for the war against those holding "Arian" views was concluded by 538 A.D.

Little horn wages war on saints

According to Daniel, the little horn power would have the same fierce qualities as its parent, the fourth beast. The little horn would become stronger than all the other horns.

It would have a mouth that spoke against the Most High and it would have eyes like a man.

As the Church became politically powerful, she became lord over the nations of Europe. It was the Church that appointed Kings and Queens. The Church decided political issues. The Church eventually ruled the world. The Church claimed the right to determine eternal life or death upon her subjects. She was as determined and cruel in conquering her foes as her pagan parent was. To expand her power and influence, the Pope promised forgiveness of sin - past, present and future along with eternal salvation to anyone willing to fight for the Holy Roman Empire. Millions perished in crusades fought in the name of God. The Roman Catholic Church conquered Europe and literally ruled with an "iron" fist for almost 13 centuries.

The Church exercised a number of spiritual prerogatives that blasphemes God's truth. For example, the Church claims infallibility for its leader! "We teach and define it to be a dogma divinely revealed that the Roman Pontiff, when he speaks *ex cathedra*, that is, when action in his office as pastor and teacher of all Christians, by his supreme Apostolic authority... he enjoys that infallibility with which the divine Redeemer willed His Church to be endowed in defining doctrine concerning faith and morals; and therefore such definitions of the said

Roman Pontiff are irreformable of themselves, and not from the consent of the Church" (Quoted from a booklet titled *The Papacy, Expression of God's Love,* page 29, published by the Knights of Columbus).

Little horn empowered 1260 years

Daniel predicted the little horn power would persecute the saints of God for a time, times and half a time. This phrase represents three and a half years. A "time" equals one year. A "times" represents two years, and "half a time" represents half a year. We know these terms represent 1260 days because John uses these time periods in an interchangeable way. See Revelation 12:6,14. If we use the day/year principle described in previous lessons, the 1260 days of the prophecy represent 1260 literal years. The day/year principle must be followed in this chapter because certain scenes in this vision correspond with the timing of the 2300 years. This point will be studied in the next lesson.

The beginning of the 1260 year period was established by Protestant reformers as 538 A.D. when the Pope began exercising authority of life and death over the subjects of the fragmented Roman empire. Absolute power as "Corrector of Heretics" had been previously granted to the Pope by Emperor Justinian through an imperial decree in 533. Giving such power to the Church set the stage for the beginning of a terrible reign of terror by Roman Pontiffs that would become known as the "dark ages."

If 538 is the correct commencement date of Papal authority, and the day/year principle is applicable, a break or termination in the power of the Papacy should occur 1260 years later in 1798. A significant number of Protestants wrote years *before* the fall of the Papacy that Church power should be broken some time in the 18th century! Writers such as Thomas Parker, 1646; Increase Mather, president of Harvard, 1723; William Burnet, 1724; and Richard Clark, 1759, and others anticipated the prophetic collapse of the Roman Church power during the 18th century!

Napoleon unwittingly fulfilled the 1260 year prophecy by capturing the Pope and putting him in prison in February, 1798. Thus the predicted 1260 years of Papal rule and persecution described by Daniel were fulfilled.

Little horn "thinks" to change law of God

Daniel predicted the little horn power would "think" to change times and laws. In 787 AD, at the Second Nicean Council, the second commandment was entirely removed from the ten commandments and the tenth commandment was divided into two separate commandments so that ten would remain. This was done so questions about the use of images or icons in worship would not come up. In addition, the fourth commandment was reduced to just a few words so questions would not be raised about the day of worship. Compare the ten commandments (Exodus 20:3-17) with a Catholic Catechism for confirmation on these changes.

Little horn claims to be God on earth

As a capstone for identification, Protestants for 400+ years have argued that the blasphemous title of the Pope, which in Latin is "Vicarious

term is used, the meaning is still the same, "in place of the Son of God."

"Anti" Christ

Historically speaking, Protestants found only one organization that met all the specifications of the little horn power of Daniel 7. It was the Papacy. (Even though there is debate within Protestantism today as to who the little horn power is, the chronological and historical harmony of the prophecy leaves no room for misinterpretation.) The point is that Satan succeeded again. He so corrupted the Christian Church that it became "anti" Christ. The Church sentenced well over 100 million people to death during its reign for

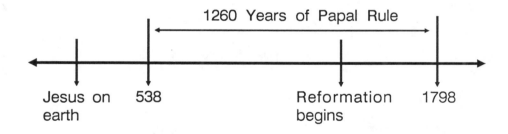

1260 Years of Papal Rule

Jesus on earth · 538 · Reformation begins · 1798

1800 years allotted to the Christians

Filii Dei", and means "in place of the Son of God", was a fulfillment of prophecy. In English, differing forms of this title are used: for example, "Vicar of Jesus Christ" or, "Vicar of God." Regardless which

refusing to receive its doctrines. For some time Satan had what he wanted all along - control of Earth! The devil has ever worked to have people worship anything or anyone but Jesus. Revelation predicts that the Antichrist (Satan himself) will yet appear on earth and claim all power and authority that rightfully belongs to God! This will be the final blasphemy! Webster defines blasphemy as "taking the prerogatives of God."

History repeated

Again, it is said that Satan is the Antichrist. He led the Jews to become antichrist during a period of 1800 years and he succeeded in causing the Christian Church to do the same in about the same length of time! In both cases, he achieved his goals by putting self-centered, ambitious and unprincipled men into leadership. Love of money and power hold far greater reward and satisfaction to the carnal nature than following the teachings of the humble and meek Carpenter from Nazareth.

Jesus starts over a final time

Jesus did not give up even though the Jews and the Christian Church became **"antichrist."** Just as He called men and women out of Judaism to begin the Christian Church, He called those who loved and sought truth out of the Christian Church to a new movement. Historically, this new organization is called the Protestant Reformation. Thus Jesus passed the responsibility of giving the gospel from the Christians to Protestants.

(Note: The term Christian as used in this review of history applies to the Roman Catholic Church which still claims to possess the one and only true Christian faith. Even though Protestants claim to be Christians, there is a vast theological difference between Catholics and Protestants.)

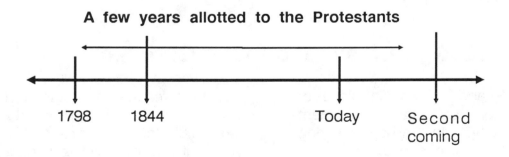

A few years allotted to the Protestants

1798   1844   Today   Second coming

"The Appointed Time of the End"

Incredible timing

The timing of prophetic events is incredible! The Catholic Church was "wounded" in 1798 when General Berthier captured the Pope and placed him in prison. The iron grip of Rome was finally broken. The Protestant Movement would rapidly grow and become a dominant world influence. Truth could now flourish. The Dark Ages were over. Jesus raised up the Protestant Movement so that men and women could hear "more" Bible truth. Truths such as salvation by faith, the ministry of Jesus in heaven instead of priestly ministry through Rome, the second coming and the prophetic meaning of 1844 are among these truths! The Roman Catholic system was brought down so that truth might prosper. Bibles could be printed and freely distributed, and freedom of worship became an inalienable right. No longer would people have to be separated from the knowledge of God by a priest. Everyone could own a Bible and have the liberty to search for truth!

Even though the point has not yet been clearly made, the contents of this lesson sets the stage for 1844 and beyond, for the Bible predicts a healing or future restoration of Papal power! (A rapid process which is being observed at this very time.) The first rise and fall of the Papacy occurred on time as predicted in Daniel and the second will be just as timely. Notice that less than 50 years separate the fall of Papal rule in 1798 and the completion of the 2,300 year prophecy in 1844. These two events are related and our next lesson will study this interesting relationship.

Summary

For 1800 years the Christian Church had an opportunity to accomplish what the Jews failed to do. But alas, the Roman Church became as evil and "anti" Christ as their predecessors the Jews. The Holy Roman Empire was brought down at the end of 1260 years in 1798 by a dictator refusing to believe in God. Even though Napoleon, like king Nebuchadnezzar, didn't know the God of heaven, history and Waterloo confirms again that there is a God that sets up kings and takes them down. (Daniel 4:25)

Jesus then raised up the Protestants. They received the responsibility to proclaim the truth of God's Word. This point is most important for somebody on earth has to be able to tell the rest of the world about "the appointed time of the end." You will see the critical reason for this point in a future lesson Looking at the pitiful condition of Protestantism today, we may be able to guess why Revelation refers to the saints at the end of the world as a "remnant."

Quiz

1. Name some of Satan's best tools to destroy the church historically.

2. Name the kingdom represented by the fourth beast:

3. Who is the little horn power that comes out of the fourth beast?

4. Who brought the little horn power down?

5. What does the title, "Vicar of God" mean?

Notes:

The Day of Judgment

Part I

Lesson 10

Comments

We have studied the failures of the Jewish nation and the Christian Church. Just as Christianity came from the cradle of Judaism, Protestantism developed within Catholicism. The force behind each movement was pursuit of truth about God. Truth needs restoration from time to time. Man becomes careless and forgets. Man-made teachings gradually displace the Word of God. Without divine light, we stumble in darkness. The farther we stray from God's Word, the darker the darkness. Inspite of the vast technological knowledge we have today, are we entering the new dark ages?

Jesus reserved the continent of North America as a haven for Protestantism. This new world discovery became a refuge for all seeking religious freedom. During the past two centuries, millions of immigrants arrived on these shores seeking religious freedom and opportunity. No one argues that God has immensely blessed this nation. But it is not the natural wealth of this country that made us great. The United States became great because she was God-fearing and lived by His principles of righteousness.

The troubles we face now are due to the fact that we have lost sight of our Creator. Like the Jews of old, we have forgotten God. As a nation, we seek pleasure more than righteousness. We love things more than we love God. We have become a nation of idolaters. TV feeds our degenerate souls by glamorizing sin a thousand times each day. Our minds are filled with meaningless and empty diversions. We never have enough money or enough time. (If you don't believe it, ask a friend for some of either!) We have become poor managers of our natural resources. Evidence all around indicates that America is headed downhill fast!

At the end of the American Revolution one of our forefathers wrote, **"The spirit of the times may alter, will alter. Our rulers will become corrupt, our people careless. A single zealot may commence persecution, and better men be his victims. It can never be too often repeated, that the time for fixing every essential right on a legal basis, is while our rulers are honest and ourselves united. From the conclusion of this war we shall be going downhill. It will not then be necessary to resort every moment to the people for their support. They will be forgotten, therefore, and their rights disregarded. They will forget themselves, and in the sole faculty of making money, they will never think of uniting to effect a due respect for their rights. The shackles, therefore, which shall not be knocked off at the conclusion of this war, will remain on us long, will be made heavier and heavier, till our rights shall revive or expire in a convulsion."**

Thomas Jefferson *Notes on Virginia*, Vol 8, page 402

Was Jefferson prophetic? Are his 200 year old remarks on target? If you think Jefferson was prophetic, Bible prophecy is even more accurate for God alone declares the end from the beginning.

Another look at Daniel 7

We need to study Daniel 7 more thoroughly because we're seeking an understanding of the importance of 1844. How can we know for sure that 1844 marks the "appointed time of the end?"

Daniel's four beasts, discussed in the last lesson, parallel the same kingdoms that Nebuchadnezzar saw. These were Babylon, Medo-Persia, Greece and Rome. Even though history removes any doubt about the identity and chronological progression of these kingdoms, Daniel 7 has information greater than the rise and fall of 4 kingdoms!

Daniel 7 contains an important key that unlocks the significance of 1844. Notice what Daniel says, **"As I looked, thrones were set in place, and the Ancient of Days took his seat. His clothing was as white as snow; the hair of his head was white like wool. His throne was flaming with fire, and its wheels were all ablaze. A river of fire was flowing, coming out from before him. Thousands upon** thousands attended him; ten thousand times ten thousand stood before him. The court was seated, and the books were opened." Daniel 7:9,10

What did Daniel see taking place in heaven? What is the meaning of this courtroom scene? Daniel saw the judgment of mankind! Reread the verses above and reflect on the following points for a moment:

1. Thrones (plural) were put in place or arranged. Heaven was made ready for a great event.

2. The Ancient of Days, the Father, presides. His appearance is greater than the brightness of the sun. His throne (compared to the other thrones) is so bright that it appears to be on fire. The glowing angels that encircle him appear to Daniel as wheels of fire.

3. This is no ordinary convention in heaven. Billions of angels throughout the universe have been summoned to this special occasion.

4. The Father takes his seat. The court was seated. And the books of record were opened.

But the scene doesn't end with these verses. There's more. Daniel says, **"In my vision at night I looked, and there before me was one like a son of man, coming with the clouds of heaven. He approached the Ancient of Days and was led into his presence. He was given authority, glory and sovereign power; all peoples, nations and men of every language worshiped him. His dominion is an everlasting dominion that will not pass away, and his kingdom is one that will never be destroyed."** Daniel 7:13,14

5. In this vast assembly of angels, Daniel sees a being that looked very different than the heavenly host. This being looked like a "son of man." Consider the significance of this. Billions of angels are gathered in this courtroom and centerstage stands a being that looks like one of the human race! This "son of man" can only be Jesus.

6. Jesus is taken before the Ancient of Days by a retinue of holy angels.

7. As Daniel watches, Jesus receives authority, glory and sovereign power.

8. Daniel concludes the vision saying that Jesus is ultimately worshiped by everyone in heaven and on earth and His kingdom will never pass away or be destroyed. (Contrast this with the 4 beasts representing kingdoms that rise and fall.)

Daniel sees the judgment of human beings

What does this scene describe? In a sentence, Daniel was permitted to see the great judgment day of the human race! The Bible speaks in many places about the judgment day as being in the future. Notice these few texts:

1. **"For God will bring every deed into judgment, including every hidden thing, whether it is good or evil."** Ecclesiastes 12:14

2. **"For he (the Father) has set a day when he will judge the world with justice by the man he has appointed..."** Acts 17:31

3. **"For we must all appear before the judgment seat of Christ, that each one may receive what is due him..."** II Corinthians 5:10

4. Peter understood that the day of judgment would be future, **"...The Lord knows how to rescue godly men from trials and to hold the unrighteous for the day of judgment..."** II Peter 2:9

5. Paul anticipated the judgment day saying, **"This will take place on the day when God will judge men's secrets through Jesus Christ..."** Romans 2:16

6. Jesus told the Pharisees that the great judgment day was in the future saying, **"The men of Nineveh will stand up at the judgment with this generation and condemn it; for they repented at the preaching of Jonah, and now one greater than Jonah is here. The Queen of the South will rise at the judgment with this generation and condemn it; for she came from the ends of the earth to listen to Solomon's wisdom, and now one greater than Solomon is here."** Matthew 12:41,42

7. Jesus told the Jews that He would someday judge them saying, **"...the Father judges no one, but has entrusted all judgment to the Son, that all may honor the Son just as they honor the Father..."** John 5:22,23

That a judgment day is prophesied in the Bible is beyond dispute. But the big question is, "When does it occur?" When does Jesus actually determine the eternal destiny of each person?

The Day of Atonement

Part of the answer to this question is found in the sanctuary service of the Old Testament! Remember, Israel faced a judgment day countdown each year. According to the Mishna, a collection of Jewish writings, the judgment of Israel began on the 1st day of the 7th month with the Feast of Trumpets and ended on the 10th day with the Day of Atonement. Today, the 10th day of the 7th month is called "Yom Kippur" which literally means, "judgment day."

If you review lesson 4, you will find an explanation of the Day of Atonement and what it meant to the Jews. In short, the Feast of Trumpets began on the 1st day of the 7th month with trumpets sounding to warn Israel that probation or mercy was closing. Each person was to search his heart and make all wrongs right before the 10th day. All sins must be transferred from the individual to the sanctuary *before* the 10th day. Failure to have sins transferred to the sanctuary meant the sinner must bear the consequence of his own deeds.

The Jews understood the Day of Atonement to be the end of the yearly judgment process. By the evening of the 9th day, all sins must be confessed and transferred into the sanctuary via the shed blood of an animal so that all sins for that year could be disposed of. On the morning of the 10th day, the sanctuary was cleansed of all accumulated sins by the High Priest. Thus the Day of Atonement was the most significant day in Jewish ceremonies. Jesus told Moses,

"...on the tenth day of the seventh month you must deny yourselves and not do any work; whether native-born or an alien living among you, because on this day atonement will be made for you, to cleanse you. Then, before the Lord, you will be clean from all your sins. It is a sabbath of rest, and you must deny yourselves; it is a lasting ordinance." Leviticus 16:29-31

Back to Daniel 7

Daniel obviously saw a courtroom setting with the Ancient of Days presiding. Daniel saw the books of record opened. The record books contain every motive, deed and thought of all that have ever lived. Each person that lived on earth will be examined and a determination for eternal life or eternal death will be made. All heaven attends this solemn meeting. Daniel mentions that ten thousand times ten thousand angels are present. Every angel anxiously watches as Jesus reviews each record and arrives at a decision that will last for eternity! It is an awesome occasion.

Note: Many people are surprised to discover in John 5:22 that Jesus is the One who makes the eternal decision upon each person. The Father has granted both the position of *advocate and judge* to Jesus. This is only fair, for Jesus has walked where we walk, He has suffered more than we suffer and He was tempted more than we are tempted. Hebrews 4:15 The beauty of this point might be understood by comparing our judicial system with heaven's judicial system. In our judicial system, we are judged by our peers. In other words, a person is judged by a jury of people having the same background as the accused. In a similar way, the people of earth are judged in heaven by one like us, a "son of man"! Daniel saw Jesus approach the Father and receive authority and sovereign power for this express purpose. Sovereign power means unlimited power.

When does the court convene?

We must find the answer to this vital question. Notice the progression of Daniel's vision. We will find several clues in Daniel 7 that associate the timing of heaven's courtroom scene with events on earth. Follow the chronology along in your own Bible:

1. Daniel was observing the violent behavior and blasphemous nature of the fourth beast when the heavenly courtroom scene began. (v7-9)
2. After court convenes in verses 9 and 10, Daniel points out that the terrible 4th beast exists until the end of the world when it is thrown into the blazing fire.

(v11) The importance of this and the sustained life of the other three beasts (lion, bear and leopard) will be seen later when we study Revelation 13.
3. Daniel's gaze returned to the courtroom scene by describing the appearing of Jesus before the Ancient of Days. Daniel points out that the Son of Man is "promoted" and given special recognition. He receives authority, glory and sovereign power and ultimately every knee bows to worship him. (v13,14)

An angel helps

Daniel was greatly troubled by this vision because of the relentless persecution of the 4th beast upon the saints. An angel is sent to Daniel with more information about the vision. Daniel is very anxious to know more about the terrible fourth beast. (v19) The angel begins by reassuring Daniel, **"The four great beasts are four kingdoms that will rise from the earth. But the saints of the Most High will receive the kingdom and will possess it forever - yes, for ever and ever."** Daniel 7:17,18

4. Daniel saw the persecution of the saints by the little horn power occur in two segments.

The first persecution continued *until* the Ancient of Days came and pronounced judgment in favor of the saints and the second persecution ends when the saints possess the kingdom. (see v21,22) We will see later that the Bible clearly predicts there are two time periods when the saints are persecuted. One is 1260 years long, the other is 1260 days long! This point will be greatly amplified in our study on Revelation 12 and 13.

5. The angel identifies the little horn power by reminding Daniel that the little horn rises out of the 4th beast and then "uprooted" three of the ten kings that took over the 4th kingdom. (Compare verses 8, 23 and 24. In our previous lesson we learned that the Papacy was able to destroy three of the ten kings that conquered Rome. These were: the Ostrogoths, the Vandals and the Heruli.)

6. The angel said the little horn power would speak against the Most High, oppress his saints and try or "think" to change set times and laws. Even worse, the saints are to be handed over to this antichrist power for a time, times and half a time. (v25)

7. In verses 26 and 27, the angel says, "But the court will sit, and the power of the little horn will be taken away and at the end, the persecuting power will be completely destroyed forever. Then all the kingdoms of earth will be given over to the saints."

Heaven's court must convene after 1798

Applying verses 21, 22 and 26 (items 4 & 7 above) we conclude that the courtroom scene takes place in heaven about the time the little horn ends the first persecution of the saints.

The time period of persecution in Daniel 7:25 is called "a time, times and half a time." This time period represents 3.5 years or 1260 days. A "time" refers to a year. Daniel 4:16,25 "Times" refers to two years, and "half a time" refers to half a year. This point is confirmed within Revelation 12:6,14. Here 1260 days and "a time, times and half a time" refer to the *same* time period and are thus interchangeable. If the time period of Daniel 7:25 is 1260 years long, the reign of Papal power from 538 to 1798, confirms this interpretation of prophecy.

Point 4 above may present a problem to some students. Some may think the little horn loses its power *because* the court sits. Don't overlook the *allotted time period* for the persecution of the saints by the little horn. In actuality, the little horn loses its power because its time of power is fulfilled when the 1260 years

---

end in 1798. Just as God set the boundaries of the oceans, he set a time limit upon the antichrist power. Daniel 7:26 can be understood to mean that the saints would be warred upon until the 1260 years of little horn's power is broken, but justice for God's people will come. The antichrist power will be destroyed forever. The blood of His persecuted saints will be avenged by Jesus Himself!

Putting the pieces together

If we combine information from Daniel 7, information from Daniel 8 and 9, information on the Day of Atonement and the texts on the day of judgment we discover four wonderful points:

1. The judgment of human beings takes place in heaven after 4 world empires have risen and fallen and after the little horn power has waged war on the saints for 1260 years.
2. Jesus is the Judge. He is granted authority, glory and sovereign power to conduct this process.
3. The restoration or cleansing of the heavenly sanctuary began at the end of the 2,300 years in 1844. Thus, 1844 marks the beginning of the appointed time of the end because the Day of Atonement marks the final stage of salvation's process in heaven. The courtroom scene can be nothing less than the judgment of human beings. It is the final event in the heavenly sanctuary. The opening of the books at this time indicates that the time to review the records of each person has come!
4. The Old Testament Day of Atonement provides valuable information that helps us understand what the cleansing of the "true" sanctuary means.

Repetition and enlargement

Understand that Daniel 7, like Daniel 2, is a broad sweeping prophecy. All details regarding the little horn power are not included in Daniel 7. There are many more things to learn that specifically relate to our day. As mentioned before, the Bible uses the process of repetition and enlargement to unfold the prophecies. Daniel 7 enlarges the details of Daniel 2. Likewise, Daniel 8 expands some of the details of Daniel 7, and we will see that the entire book of Revelation enlarges upon Daniel 8-12!

The process of the judgment examined

What happens in the judgment process? How are we judged? Solomon, the wise man, wrote,

"...here is the conclusion of the matter: **Fear God and keep his commandments, for this is the whole duty of man. For God will bring every deed into judgment, including every hidden thing, whether it is good or evil.**" Ecclesiastes 12:13,14

In 1844, Jesus began cleansing the sanctuary in heaven. What defiled the heavenly sanctuary? The recorded sins of people on earth. Remember how the sins of Israel were transferred to the earthly sanctuary each day so that it had to be cleansed each year on the Day of Atonement? So the sins of each person are accurately and fully recorded in heaven's sanctuary. Those who lived up to all the knowledge they had were given the righteousness of Christ. This is the mystery of God! This is how the plan of salvation can save the most vile offender! In 1844, Jesus began going through the books of record. This process is conducted before the host of angels so that nothing is hidden. Jesus thoroughly investigates all aspects of each person's life that lived upon earth. He began with the first to die, a man called Abel.

As Jesus proceeds through the books of record, He makes an irrevocable decision about each person regarding eternal life or death. Those in the books of record who rejected the promptings of the Holy Spirit are lost. They stand condemned as "uncovered" sinners before the Father. They refused to live by faith and they refused to heed the promptings of the Holy Spirit. Understand that Jesus intimately investigates every aspect of a person's life to insure that a fair decision is made. Jesus considers what each person knew, what each person had opportunity to know, what each person did with what he knew or believed. He also considers where each person came from, their time and place, how each person treated others and many, many other factors. This is a solemn scene of eternal importance. Millions of reverent angels are in attendance.

In 1844, the judgment of the dead began. This process has been going on in heaven for almost 150 years. Soon, the judgment of the living will begin! The work in heaven will turn from the books of records to the lives of the living! We'll learn more about this in lessons 14 and 15.

A new problem arises

If the judgment of the dead began in 1844, what happened to all those people who died and went to heaven or hell before 1844? In other words, how could eternal judgment be passed upon people who died centuries ago if the judgment process did not begin until 1844?

Many people believe that the sentence of eternal life or of eternally burning in hell is executed at death. Naturally, such a thinking would require that judgment be made at the time of death. Is this what the Bible teaches about the judgment of mankind? No. The Bible clearly says that God has appointed a certain time to judge the world. Acts 17:31 In Daniel, it's called "the appointed time of the end." 1844 marks the beginning of this time period, for this is when Jesus begins to cleanse the heavenly sanctuary. In fact, when Jesus returns at the second coming, He brings His reward with Him indicating that the judgment process is completed! **"Behold I am coming soon! My reward is with me, and I will give to everyone according to what he has done."** Revelation 22:12

Does God burn people for eternity?

Through the centuries, Satan has tormented millions of people with the concept that when a person dies, he goes straight to heaven or hell. Many Christians accept this idea today and aren't particularly bothered by it. After all, no one has seen a large pit of fire where loved ones are burning and writhing in pain.

Only in the past century has this doctrine lost most of its terror. In Protestantism today, almost everyone goes to heaven. When was the last time you heard a funeral sermon sending someone to hell?

The doctrine of an eternally burning hell has a terrible history. This teaching was used by the Roman Church to control the masses. The people who lived during the Dark Ages didn't have Bibles, so they lived in constant fear and had many superstitions about God. (For example, a sneeze was believed to be a demon attempting to snatch away one's breath. Thus the quick response "bless you" was offered since last rites were necessary for salvation.) The superstitious fear of the people was preyed upon by Roman clerics as a way of raising money. Families could both buy deceased loved ones out of the torment of purgatory and purchase eternal life for themselves, regardless of any behavior. The wealthier the family, the higher the price of course. (In fact, the construction of St. Peter's Basilica was financed entirely from the sale of indulgences in the 15th and 16th centuries. An indulgence was a "legal document" from the Pope granting eternal life without first going to purgatory.)

Protestants in general still hold to the teaching of the immortality of the soul. There are several problems with the idea that one goes to heaven or hell at death. These are:

1. First, the Bible does not say that burning forever in hell fire is the penalty for sin. On the contrary, the Bible says that, **"...the wages of sin is death."** Romans 6:23

2. If burning in hell forever is the penalty for sin, then Jesus could not have possibly paid the penalty for sin by dying on Calvary for He was resurrected the third day.

3. Going to heaven or hell at the time of death presupposes an immediate judgment decision upon that individual. From Daniel 7 and 8 we learned that the court did not convene until 1844. Decisions for eternal life or death were not made before that time!

4. If people go to heaven or hell immediately at death, then what is the purpose of the resurrection? Notice that the wicked and the righteous are both resurrected. Paul said, **"And I have the same hope in God as these men, that there will be a resurrection of both the righteous and the wicked."** Acts 24:15
    Some suggest the purpose of the resurrection is to come back and get the earthly body. According to Paul, we won't be able to use the earthly body which is perishable! **"I declare to you, brothers, that flesh and blood cannot inherit the kingdom of God, nor does the perishable inherit the imperishable... the dead will be raised imperishable, and we will be changed. For the perishable must clothe itself with the imperishable, and the mortal with immortality."** I Corinthians 15:50, 52, 53

5. Jesus clearly predicts two resurrections, **"...for a time is coming when all who are in their graves will hear his voice and come out - those who have done good will rise to live, and those who have done evil will rise to be condemned."** John 5:28,29 If people are burning in hell, why would they be resurrected too? Wouldn't that be a case of being condemned before proven innocent?

6. John saw the redeemed awake from death at the second coming. He says, **"...they came to life and reigned with Christ a thousand years."** Revelation 20:4

Death is like sleep

Fifty-three times in the New Testament, death is called sleep. Death is simply a condition of unconsciousness. Solomon says, **"For the living know that they will die, but the dead know nothing; they have no further reward, and even the memory of them is forgotten. Their love, their hate and their** jealousy have long since vanished; never again will they have a part in anything that happens under the sun." Ecclesiastes 9:5,6

Jesus said to His disciples concerning Lazarus, "...our friend Lazarus has fallen asleep; but I am going there to wake him up. His disciples replied 'Lord, if he sleeps, he will get better.' Jesus had been speaking of his death, but his disciples thought he meant natural sleep. So then he told them plainly, 'Lazarus is dead.'" John 11:11-14

When Jesus resurrected Lazarus from death, Lazarus gave no report of stoking fires in hell or dancing in heaven. No! He'd been sleeping and thus unconscious of anything going on!

In our next lesson, we'll look at the story of the rich man and Lazarus. Does it prove people are burning in hell?

Summary

We have chronologically located the Day of Judgment described by Daniel. The date is 1844. The courtroom is in heaven. It is the heavenly Day of Atonement to which the wilderness Day of Atonement pointed forward. Since that time, Jesus, Judge of Mankind, has been involved with determining the eternal destiny of each person as the books of record are reviewed. The books

clearly reveal the choices that each person made. The record books contain what the person knew at the time, what they did and why! Everything is exposed in the judgment.

At the second coming, those who have been granted eternal life will rise in the first resurrection. Later, those who have done evil will rise to meet their Maker and receive their due reward at the end of the millennium. We shall continue our investigation of these things in the next lesson.

Quiz

1. Who came before the Ancient of Days. What did He receive?

2. Daniel was told the little horn power would persecute the saints for:

3. Give one reason why the judgment day must precede the second coming:

4. What is the wages of sin?

5. How many times does the NT refer to death as sleep?

The Day of Judgment

Part II

Lesson 11

Review

From Daniel, we learned that the judgment of the human race began in 1844. The great courtroom scene began with the Ancient of Days taking His seat. The books of record were opened and a review of each person who had died commenced.

The importance of 1844 will develop even further as we continue our study in Revelation. However, the fundamental issue of what happens to a person when he dies must be addressed because death, judgment and reward are connected. The truth on this subject is very impor-

tant, for it is directly connected to the climactic story of Revelation!

A number of the Eastern Mystic religions believe in the transmigration of the soul. This concept teaches that the soul was once a lower form of life before entering the human being, and at death, life moves on to a higher or lower form depending on how one lived in this life. Many Christians have a theology that parallels this concept. The basic difference between Christians and those believing in the transmigration of the soul is that Christians believe life *begins* with conception in the womb. On the other hand, many Christians and Eastern Mystic religions believe the soul is immortal and thus not subject to death. Both ideas are plainly contrary to the scriptures. The soul can die! God says, **"...the soul who sins is the**

one who will die." Ezekiel 18:4 If the soul is immortal, when is immortality bestowed upon it?

When does life begin?

The Bible tells us, **"And the Lord God formed man from the dust of the ground and breathed into his nostrils the breath of life, and man became a living being."** Genesis 2:7

A living being is a combination of two elements: the body and the breath (power) of life. Separate these two elements, and you don't have a living being! Life may be thought of as light. Connect a light bulb with electricity and there is light. Separate the electricity from the bulb and there is no light.

Some people believe that when a person dies, the spirit (the soul) returns to God. Solomon said, **"Remember him (our Creator) - before the silver cord is severed, or the golden bowl is broken; before the pitcher is shattered at the spring, or the wheel broken at the well, and the dust returns to the ground it came from, and the spirit returns to God who gave it."** Ecclesiastes 12:6,7 From this scripture, it is clear that the spirit returns to God who gave it. This is true of *both* the righteous and the wicked! The word translated spirit in Ecclesiastes 12:6,7 is the identical word used for breath in Job

27:3. Notice what Job said, **"...as long as I have life within me, the breath of God in my nostrils, my lips will not speak wickedness..."** Job 27:3,4 In other words, what returns to God is the power to live.

God grants breath to all that live. This is true of animals and man. Of Noah's flood it is said, **"Every living thing that moved on the earth perished - birds, livestock, wild animals, all the creatures that swarm over the earth, and all mankind. Everything on dry land that had the breath of life in its nostrils died."** Genesis 7:21,22

The Greek and Hebrew words for spirit mean wind or breath. The Hebrew word, "ruach" and the Greek word, "pneuma" do not refer to some intelligent entity free of the body. Rather, these words simply apply to the breath of life. The word for breath is often translated spirit and vice versa. The point is that a soul does not exist when the spirit or breath is separated from the body! When breath and a body are brought together, the result is a soul. Our example of the light bulb demonstrated this. When power is applied to the bulb we have light. When power is disconnected, there is no light. In the same way, when the breath of life is connected to a body, we have an intelligent soul - whether animal or man. When the breath of life is taken from the body, there is no soul.

The Hebrew word for soul is "nephesh" and the Greek word is "psuche." Both of these words mean or imply that a living being is a soul! Solomon wrote, **"Man's fate is like that of the animals; the same fate awaits them both: As one dies, so dies the other. All have the same breath (spirit), man has no advantage over the animal..."** Ecclesiastes 3:19

Other Bible writers agree

Adam and Eve were expressly driven from their Eden home so that they could not eat from the tree of life and live forever! After Adam and Eve sinned, Jesus said, **"...the man has now become like one of us, knowing good and evil. He must not be allowed to reach out his hand and take also from the tree of life and eat, and live forever."** Genesis 3:22 The point here is that Adam and Eve were removed from the Garden of Eden for the express purpose of death. As long as they could eat of the tree of life, they would live. So they had to be removed from the garden.

The Bible says that the ability to exist forever comes only through Jesus. John says, **"He who has the Son has life; he who does not have the Son of God does not have life."** 1 John 5:12

In Paul's day, many of the early Christians sorrowed thinking there was no resurrection - no life hereafter. To set the matter straight, Paul said, **"According to the Lord's own word, we tell you that we who are still alive, who are left till the coming of the Lord, will certainly not precede those who have fallen asleep. For the Lord himself will come down from heaven, with a loud command, with the voice of the archangel and with the trumpet call of God, and the dead in Christ will rise first. After that, we who are still alive and are left will be caught up with them in the clouds to meet the Lord in the air... Therefore encourage each other with these words."** I Thessalonians 4:15-18 Paul did not comfort those grieving for their deceased friends with the notion their friends were in heaven. No. He pointed them forward to the resurrection.

The devil started it

The one who brought confusion to this point in the very beginning was the devil. Satan told Eve she wouldn't die if she disobeyed God. Today, Satan has twisted the meaning of death 180 degrees so that many people believe that death means life! King David knew the dead weren't in heaven praising the Lord for he said, **"It is not the dead who praise the Lord, those who go down to silence; it is we who extol the Lord..."** Psalm 115:17

The apostle Peter also knew the dead weren't in heaven praising the Lord. In his famous sermon on the Day of Pentecost he quoted a number of references from the Old Testament where king David had prophesied about the coming Messiah. Then Peter concluded by saying that David was not in heaven. He said, **"Brothers, I can tell you confidently that the patriarch David died and was buried, and his tomb is here to this day... For David did not ascend to heaven, and yet he said, 'The Lord said to my Lord: Sit at my right hand until I make your enemies a footstool for your feet.' "** Acts 2:29,34

King David knew the dead were not in heaven playing a harp and singing praises to God. He wrote, **"No one remembers you (God) when he is dead. Who praises you from the grave?."** Psalm 6:5 Solomon understood death just like his father, David. He wrote, **"Whatever your hand finds to do, do it with all your might, for in the grave, where you are going, there is neither working nor planning nor knowledge nor wisdom."** Ecclesiastes 9:10

Daniel saw the great resurrection at the end of time. He clearly states that some of the dead will awake to everlasting life and others will awake to shame and everlasting contempt. **"Multitudes who sleep in the dust of the earth will awake: some to everlasting life, others to shame and everlasting contempt."** Daniel 12:2

There is consistent harmony throughout the Bible on the nature of death. Man is mortal and death is like sleep. Man is unconscious of anything that goes on. The dead are dead! The dead simply remain in a state of unconsciousness. They rest from their labors until the resurrection morning.

(The author once visited with a man that claimed to have died on the operating table for 5 minutes. He reported that he had an out-of-body experience in bright lights. Does a hallucinogenic experience validate or invalidate the scriptures?)

What about mediums?

Jesus clearly told the Jews to have nothing to do with mediums or spiritists. These are people who practice and promote communication with the dead. Jesus said, **"Do not turn to mediums or seek out spiritists, for you will be defiled by them... A man or woman who is a medium or spiritist among you must be put to death. You are to stone them; their blood will be on their own heads."** Leviticus 19:31, 20:27

King Saul finds an unhappy medium

A special story is preserved in the Bible to demonstrate 3 important things. It's conclusion is found in I Samuel 28. In brief, King Saul, the first king of Israel, had repeatedly failed to obey the Lord. He was disobedient and rebellious. One day Samuel was sent to Saul telling him the kingdom would be taken from him and given to another. That promised "other" was a young shepherd boy named David. Saul remembered these words from time to time. Time passed, and Samuel died.

One day the Philistines assembled at Shunem to fight the Israelites. When Saul saw the size of their army, he became afraid and terror filled his heart. The Bible tells the rest of the story, **"He inquired of the Lord, but the Lord did not answer him by dreams or Urim or prophets. Saul then said to his attendants, 'Find me a woman who is a medium, so I may go and inquire of her.' 'There is one in Endor,' they said. So Saul disguised himself, putting on other clothes, and at night he and two men went to the woman.**

'Consult a spirit for me,' he said 'and bring up for me the one I name.' But the woman said to him, 'Surely you know what Saul has done. He has cut off the mediums and spiritists from the land. Why have you set a trap for my life to bring about my death?'

Saul swore to her by the Lord, 'As surely as the Lord lives, you will not be punished for this.' Then the woman asked, 'Whom shall I bring up for you?' 'Bring up Samuel,' he said. When the woman saw Samuel, she cried out of the top of her voice to Saul and said, 'Why have you deceived me? You are Saul!'

The king said to her, 'Don't be afraid. What do you see?' The woman said, 'I see a spirit coming up out of the ground.' 'What does he look like?' he asked. 'An old man wearing a robe is coming up,' she said. Then Saul knew it was Samuel, and he bowed down and prostrated himself with his face to the ground.

Samuel said to Saul 'Why have you disturbed me by bringing me up?' 'I am in great distress' Saul said. 'The Philistines are fighting against me and God has turned away from me. He no longer answers me, either by prophets or by dreams. So I have called on you to tell me what to do.'

Samuel said 'Why do you consult me, now that the Lord has turned away from you and become your enemy? The Lord has done what he predicted through me. The Lord has torn the kingdom out of your hands and given it to one

of your neighbors - to David. Because you did not obey the Lord or carry out his fierce wrath against the Amalekites, the Lord has done this to you today. The Lord will hand over both Israel and you to the Philistines, and tomorrow you and your sons will be with me. The Lord will also hand over the army of Israel to the Philistines.'

Immediately, Saul fell full length on the ground, filled with fear because of Samuel's words..."
I Samuel 28:6-20

Three important points are made:

1. The Lord had turned his back on Saul and refused to answer him by prophets or dreams. Neither did the Lord answer Saul through the medium of Endor. In his desperation, Saul sought out the devil. What he saw and heard was a demon in the form of Samuel the deceased prophet.

2. Notice that Satan's remarks were quite accurate about Saul's condition. Even though Satan doesn't precisely know the future (he is not omniscient), he is very smart. He had carefully studied Saul and in the medium's house he succeeded in destroying whatever courage the abandoned king may have had.

3. Satan clearly gave Saul the idea that Samuel was in the grave (not in heaven or in hell) and that he would soon join Samuel in death.

The doctrine that deceased people are in heaven or hell opens the door to communication with spirits. The Bible is absolutely clear that such communication is not with angelic beings but with demons.

Jesus - now alive forever and ever

In Revelation, Jesus told John, "**...do not be afraid. I am the First and the Last. I am the Living One; I was dead, and behold I am alive for ever and ever! And I hold the keys of death and Hades (the grave).**" Revelation 1:17,18 Jesus clearly holds the keys to death and the grave. He has the power of life within Himself! Jesus will use the keys of death and open the graves of the righteous at the resurrection during the second coming. Paul said, "**For the Lord Himself will come down from heaven, with a loud command, with the voice of the archangel and with the trumpet call of God, and the dead in Christ will rise first. After that, we who are still alive and are left will be caught up with them in the clouds to meet the Lord in the air. And so we will be with the Lord forever.**" I Thessalonians 4:16, 17

Problem texts

There are two texts in the Bible that can be particularly confusing on the matter of death. We'll look at these briefly:

"For Christ died for sins once for all, the righteous for the unrighteous, to bring you to God. He was put to death in the body but made alive by the Spirit through whom also he went and preached to the spirits in prison who disobeyed long ago when God waited patiently in the days of Noah while the ark was being built..." I Peter 3:18-20

Some people interpret this text to mean that Jesus, during the time He was dead, went to a prison where evil people had been held since the flood and there preached forgiveness to them.

Such a view opens up insurmountable questions. For example, after a person is once consigned to hell, can he be set free? The Roman Church taught for centuries that freedom from hell was possible for a contribution to the Church. But look at the flip side of the coin. Suppose you were in heaven and for a fee, you could be sent to hell by someone that didn't like you? As you quickly see, the actions of other people cannot determine nor control your eternal destiny whether in heaven or hell.

Consider this too. What would be the point of Jesus preaching forgiveness to people who had been burning in hell for 2,000 years? Can they now repent and go to heaven? Jesus preaching repentance to someone burning in hell for 2,000 is anticlimactic isn't it? How persuasive would Jesus (or anyone for that matter) have to be to persuade those burning in hell for 2,000 years that they need to repent? The whole idea is absurd. The Bible teaches that we have only one chance for salvation. It is during this life. Hebrews 4:7

Peter, in our problem text, is making the point that Jesus was put to death in the body and made alive by the Spirit of God. By this *same Spirit,* Jesus patiently waited for 120 years in the days of Noah to save any and all who would get on board. (See Genesis 6:1-8) Then Peter says, **"For this is the reason the gospel was preached even to those who are now dead, so that they might be judged according to men in regard to the body, but live according to God in regard to the spirit."** I Peter 4:6 In other words, Peter says the gospel is preached to those who are now dead to spiritual things (the Jews) so they might see their need to live in harmony with the spirit and receive life and the approval of God! The true meaning of I Peter 3 does not conflict with other scriptures on death when rightly understood.

There is harmony in the sum of the parts!

The rich man and Lazarus

No parable has caused more discussion than this one. Luke records the story, **"There was a rich man who was dressed in purple and fine linen and lived in luxury every day. At his gate was laid a beggar named Lazarus, covered with sores and longing to eat what fell from the rich man's table. Even the dogs came and licked his sores. The time came when the beggar died and the angels carried him to Abraham's side. The rich man also died and was buried.**

In hell, where he was in torment, he looked up and saw Abraham far away, with Lazarus by his side. So he called to him, 'Father Abraham, have pity on me and send Lazarus to dip the tip of his finger in water and cool my tongue, because I am in agony in this fire.' But Abraham replied, 'Son, remember that in your lifetime you received your good things, while Lazarus received bad things, but now he is comforted here and you are in agony. And besides all this, between us and you a great chasm has been fixed, so that those who want to go from here to you cannot, nor can anyone cross over from there to us.'

He answered, 'Then I beg you, father, send Lazarus to my father's house, for I have five brothers. Let him warn them, so that they will not also come to this place of torment.' Abraham replied, 'They have Moses and the Prophets; let them listen to them.' 'No, father Abraham,' he said, 'but if someone from the dead goes to them, they will repent.' He said to him, 'If they do not listen to Moses and the Prophets, they will not be convinced even if someone rises from the dead.'" Luke 16:19-31

A casual look at the story raises several questions:

1. Assuming there are people in heaven and hell, can they actually carry on a conversation?
2. Can people in heaven carry water to those in hell?
3. Do the rich go to hell and the poor go to heaven?

Josephus, a Jewish historian who lived shortly after Christ, tells us this story was in vogue at the time of Christ. It's a tale of theological contrasts within Judaism. For example, the Sadducees rejected the idea of a resurrection believing that one went straight to their eternal reward at death while the Pharisees believed in the resurrection. (See Acts 23:6-9) The Pharisees believed a wealthy person was blessed of God for his righteousness while a poor person was rewarded for some evil, either hidden or hereditary. See John 9.

Jesus took this well-known tale of many opposites and tied it together with some very important points - none of which has to do with burning in hell or dancing in heaven. Notice:

1. The Jews were wealthy. They had been given God's richest blessings. They had been enlightened with truth. They had been chosen as a special people.

2. The poor Gentiles did not have the opportunities of the Jews. But circumstances do change! The Jews would become destitute and the Gentiles would become enlightened! (Remember the end of the 490 years, 34 A.D.?)

3. With roles and opportunities exchanged, the converted Jew in torment cries out to the Gentile in heaven, **"I have 5 brothers. Go warn them of things to come." "Abraham replied, 'They have Moses and the Prophets; let them listen to them.' 'No, father Abraham,' he said, 'but if someone from the dead goes to them, they will repent.' He said to him, 'If they do not listen to Moses and the Prophets, they will not be convinced even if someone rises from the dead.' "** Luke 16:19-31

Jesus concludes the tale by placing Himself in the heart of the story saying, "even if someone rises from the dead, they will not be convinced - they are that hard-hearted."

Like Peter's vision of the unclean animals, the story of the rich man and Lazarus is designed to teach an important lesson. It is not designed to confirm a theological point. As we have seen in this series of studies, the Bible offers a consistent message. It's inspiration comes from One that changes not.

The destiny of the wicked

Since the Bible says burning in hell forever is not the penalty of sin, what is the penalty of sin? The Bible says, **"...the wages of sin is death."** The Bible clearly says there will be a hell fire! **"...but fire came down from heaven and devoured them. And the devil, who deceived them, was thrown into the lake of burning sulfur...."** Revelation 20:9,10

Malachi, the Old Testament prophet, saw the total destruction of the wicked. He writes, **" 'Surely the day is coming; it will burn like a furnace. All the arrogant and every evildoer will be stubble, and that day that is coming will set them on fire,' says the Lord Almighty. 'Not a root or a branch will be** left to them. But for you who revere my name, the sun of righteousness will rise with healing in its wings. And you will go out and leap like calves released from the stall. Then you will trample down the wicked; they will be ashes under the soles of your feet on the day when I do these things,' says the Lord Almighty." Malachi 4:1-3

Two more difficult texts

Revelation 20:10 says, "...they will be tormented day and night for ever and ever." and Revelation 14:11 says, "...and the smoke of their torment rises for ever and ever..."

Do these texts imply an eternally burning hell? At first glance they seem to! Will Jesus burn and scorch people for ever and ever? Is this the unquenchable wrath of God?

First, we have determined that the wages of sin is death. Death, by definition of many Bible writers, means sleep or a state of unconsciousness. The destruction of the wicked cannot last eternally because in this scenario, they would never die, thus the penalty of sin is never paid.

The second text (Revelation 14:11) literally indicates that the smoke from the destruction of the wicked rises for ever and ever. If the complete destruction of the wicked means an end to sin and sinners, the scriptures then indicates that the smoke of their torment can not be put out. The lake of fire will consume sin and sinners until nothing remains.

Revelation 20:10 seems to say on the surface that the wicked are tormented day and night eternally. Actually though, John was expressing two important ideas. First, sinners burn differing lengths of time and secondly, while they burn, they feel the torment of their suffering.

From Malachi 4 we know the wicked will be eventually reduced to ashes. From John, we know the wicked will be burned up and that there will be a new heaven and a new earth for the first earth is passed away! Revelation 21:1 From II Peter 3 we know the earth and everything in it will melt and be laid bare with great heat. From the weight of all Bible evidence, John's comments in Revelation 20:10 indicating the wicked are tormented day and night forever can be interpreted to mean "as long as they exist." Like marriage (forgive the comparison), the vow lasts forever as long as both parties live.

Hell fire is not the greatest punishment

In a later lesson, we will study the sequence of events that take place before the final destruction. We will look further into the resurrections and the final death.

But the greatest punishment that Jesus gives to His created beings at the very end is not hell fire. Rather, the greatest punishment placed upon the wicked at the end of the millennium is a revelation of God's tender love for each person. Here's the story:

1. At the second coming, the saints are taken to heaven and the wicked remaining upon the earth are slain by the brightness of Jesus' glory. The earth is desolated by the splendor of righteousness!

2. The saints (the resurrected and the living) are caught up with Jesus in the air and they return to heaven for 1000 years. The purpose of this 1000 years is very simple: Jesus wants each redeemed person to clearly see that His decision on those not in heaven was fair. In other words, the saints now get to review the books of record. They learn, first hand, why a loved one or friend was not granted eternal life. Every mystery will be laid open. After reviewing each case to their satisfaction, all the saints are convinced that Jesus was loving, just and merciful in His judgment on each person.

3. At the end of the 1000 years, the saints return to earth with Jesus. Jesus resurrects the wicked. They come forth to gaze upon the New Jerusalem and the saints within the city. Satan, who was bound to the desolate earth, now stirs the wicked to attack the New Jerusalem and rob the redeemed of their home. As the mob rushes toward the city, Jesus stops the vast throng just as he commanded the storm on Galilee to be still.

4. Then every eye is drawn to the sky where a great panorama of salvation's story is played. Each person (saints and sinners) watches the drama, for the most incredible event to ever happen is now to take place. The giant screen-play in the heaven not only tells the big story of God's love, it replays each person's life before its owner. Both saint and sinner stand in awe. Now they see as never before the extended mercy of salvation - the mystery of God. Now they comprehend what they dimly understood before. Now the saints see the humility of Jesus and sinners see Paradise lost. The wicked behold the One who loved them beyond understanding, the One who died that they might have the opportunity of salvation!

5. Every knee bows before Jesus, the Father and the Holy Spirit. They are righteous. They are fair. They are love! The wicked bow before their justice. The saints bow before their mercy. Now, at this grand moment, before all human beings that ever lived, the 7th and final seal is broken on the book of life. The book is opened. Now the multitude beyond number understand a new dimension about God. He foreknew all this. His written record, sealed before the world was created, is *exactly* the same as the story contained in the books of record and reviewed in the sky!

6. Now God is exonerated before His creatures. God has been proven as a God of love. He freely granted His creatures the power of choice. Now, Satan stands before the vast multitude as a despicable liar. The evidence clearly shows that God does not use His foreknowledge to manipulate or control the outcome of any event. His creatures truly have the greatest power outside of divinity: the power of choice.

The saints rejoice with unbounding joy at the choices they made: the choice to live by faith, the choice to follow Jesus, the choice to struggle against sin, the choice to be what Jesus wanted them to be, the choice to do what He wanted, and the choice to go wherever He directed!

On the other hand, sinners are crushed. In despair beyond words they see the tragic result of their choices. They look upon the Holy City, Jesus and the saints and a grief beyond comprehension overtakes them. They have no anger against the Godhead. They are love and the wicked stand before God with regret beyond understanding. Their regret is not based on heart-felt repentance, rather, it is based on the consequence of seeing what they have lost. The seeds of rebellion are so deep that repentance is impossible. In agony beyond description they turn upon each other to vent their anguish. In mercy, Jesus sends fire down from heaven and ends the nightmare.

Quiz

1. When does man become a living soul?

2. When an evil person dies, what returns to God.

3. See if you can find two scriptures in this lesson that call death "sleep":

4. What does God say about mediums?

5. Can demons personate dead people?

Notes:

Notes:

Introduction to Revelation

Lesson 12

Comments

The book of Revelation may be likened to the fuse box in your house. As all wires meet and end in the fuse box, so all books of the Bible meet and end in Revelation. Revelation can only be understood with the help of other scripture. One authority states that Revelation makes more than 500 allusions to the Old Testament!

Because Revelation's story is connected to all the books in the Bible and because we have to understand certain things before we can interpret Revelation, we have had to spend time exploring these four essential doctrines:

1. The second coming of Jesus
2. Salvation by faith
3. The work of Jesus in the heavenly sanctuary
4. The state of the dead

One more essential doctrine remains: the truth about worship. Revelation predicts that all the world will worship the great Antichrist that shall appear on earth, "except those whose names are written in the book of life!" Why the world will worship the Antichrist will be explored in this volume.

For now, we need to begin looking into Revelation's story and learning the meaning of the things written there. Notice that Revelation offers a reward to all that study the book: **"Blessed is the one who reads the words of this prophecy, and blessed are those who hear it and take to heart what is written in it, because the time is near."** Revelation 1:3 Remember from lesson 2, when a prophecy becomes applicable, its language becomes applicable. A special blessing now belongs to those who study Revelation because the appointed time is near!

A very logical sequence

Revelation follows a very decided progression in its story. Notice the outline:

Story	Chapter
Introduction	1
7 Churches	2-3
Jesus given book with 7 seals	4-5
Jesus opens 7 seals	6-8
Great multitude is redeemed	7
7 Trumpets	8-11
2 Witnesses	11
Satan's origin and work	12
Rise of Babylon	13
Personal appearance of Satan	13
3 Warning messages	14
7 Last plagues	15-16
Last moments of Babylon	17
Collapse of Babylon	18
Second coming	19
End of 1000 years	20
New Jerusalem	21
Eternal life	22

As you already know, the gospel story is not hard to understand. (After all, 5+ billion people must hear it and understand it!) The basic issues within Revelation are not hard to comprehend either. The hardest part of understanding Revelation is getting a handle on the cryptic language.

Revelation is coded with three types of language. These are:

1. Symbolic or spiritual language
2. Analogue or analogous language
3. Literal language and terms

These three language types are mixed throughout the book and discerning whether language is literal, symbolic or analogous can be difficult. Let's observe some samples of each language type:

1. Symbolic language

"...There I saw a woman sitting on a scarlet beast that was covered with blasphemous names and had seven heads and ten horns... This title was written on her forehead: Mystery, Babylon the Great, The Mother of Prostitutes and of the Abominations of the Earth." Revelation 17:3, 5

Who is the woman wearing the title Babylon? The Bible says, "The woman you saw is the great city that rules over the kings of the earth." Revelation 17:18

Very important point: If the student suspects the language to be symbolic, a relevant text must clearly define the symbol. The key word here is "relevant." A symbol can have different meanings at different times! (Compare Revelation 12:9 with Numbers 21:9 & John 3:14)

Another example of symbolic language: **"Their bodies (2 witnesses) will lie in the street of the great city, which is figuratively called Sodom and Egypt, where also their Lord was crucified."** Revelation 11:8

It is a historical fact that Jesus was not crucified in Sodom or in Egypt. He was crucified outside Jerusalem. Revelation predicts the two witnesses will lie in the street of "the great city." From Rev 17:18 we learn who the great city is. It is the harlot, Babylon.

Babylon will be just like Sodom and Egypt. Sodom represents unrestrained evil passions and Egypt represents hardness of heart (as manifested by Pharaoh). Both Sodom and Egypt passed the point of no return - they committed the unpardonable sin. Babylon will do the same. Babylon will war against the saints, kill the two witnesses and think they have done God a favor. The Jews and Romans crucified Jesus in this same state of mind!

2. Analogous language

"The locusts looked like horses prepared for battle. On their heads they wore something like crowns of gold, and their faces resembled human faces." Rev 9:7

The important point to notice here, is the comparison or analogy. The locusts looked like horses, but they aren't horses! They don't symbolize horses either, for if they did, the scripture would clearly define the meaning of the symbol with relevant scripture.

3. Literal language

"And I saw a beast coming out of the sea. He had ten horns and seven heads... and on each head a blasphemous name." Revelation 13:1

The number 10 and the number 7 are literal. John clearly saw 10 horns and 7 heads. The horns and heads are symbolic for they are discussed and explained in Revelation 17. Numbers in Bible prophecy are always literal and real. What they refer to may be symbolic. In this case the heads and horns are symbolic because the symbols are later explained.

Sometimes mixed up

One thing that makes interpretation difficult is that language types are sometimes mixed in the same sentence! Notice this one:

"The great city split into three parts, and the cities of the nations collapsed..." Revelation 16:19 Remember the verse used earlier? **"The woman you saw is the great city that rules over the kings of the earth."** Revelation 17:18 This woman is the great prostitute that rules over the nations. Revelation 17:3-6

From 17:18 we learned that the "great city" is the woman called Babylon. In 16:19, we learned that the great city (symbolically Babylon) is split into three parts at the second coming of Jesus while the (literal) cities of the nations collapsed.

How can we tell which type of language is being used? How can we know if a term is literal, symbolic or analogous? Since mixing or using terms can result in bizarre interpretations, we must be very careful. We need a set of rules to govern our methods of interpretation.

Rules of interpretation

The rules we use for interpretation of Revelation naturally affect our conclusions. Anytime we change the rules, we change the conclusions. Since the Bible does not specifically state the rules of interpretation, we must scan the Bible to discover certain principles of prophetic interpretation that are trustworthy. The first step in this process is to identify the various types of prophecy:

Five types of prophecy

The Bible presents a minimum of five types of prophecy. These include:

1. Messianic prophecies

These prophecies specifically relate to the person of Jesus in either His first or second coming. Two examples of Messianic prophecy are found in Isaiah 53 and Psalm 22.

2. Judaic prophecies

These prophecies predicted the prosperity or destruction of Israel. Promises and threatenings are alike included. These prophecies have conditional elements in them most of the time. A good example of this type of prophecy is found in Deuteronomy 28. These prophecies contain important object lessons for all generations of people, for God's beneficent relationship with man is clearly revealed.

3. Day of the Lord prophecies

These prophecies are scattered throughout scripture and relate to the vindication of God and/or His people. These prophecies often have parallel applications for they demonstrate the wrath of God and/or the vindication of His people in a contemporary setting as well as at a future time. For example, Isaiah 24 and Ezekiel 7 can be seen as parallels of final days of Israel's history and the earth's history. Sometimes, "Day of the Lord" prophecies have conditional elements embedded in them.

Matthew 24 is also considered to be a "Day of the Lord" prophecy. The prophecy concerning the end of Jerusalem in 70 A.D. and the end of the world are mingled together because there are ominous parallels.

4. Local prophecies

Local prophecies apply to specific people, places and times. For example, the prophecy concerning Nineveh is a local prophecy. Local prophecies usually require a "local prophet" or messenger to explain or proclaim the prophecy. In the case of Nineveh, Jonah was the local prophet.

5. Apocalyptic prophecies

Apocalyptic prophecy is defined as structural prophecy; that is, prophecy that outlines a specific sequence of events that relates to or culminates with the end of the world. Both the fulfillment and sequence of apocalyptic prophecy are unconditional. A clear example of this type prophecy can be found in Daniel 2. Nebuchadnezzar's dream outlined a sequence of kingdoms. In Revelation, sequence and structure are defined by numeric order; i.e., trumpet 2 occurs *after* trumpet 1, etc.

Apocalyptic prophecies sometimes have conditional elements within their structure relating to fulfillment. For example, the winds of destruction are held back in Revelation 7:3 until the servants of God are sealed. That the winds will blow is unconditional; *when* they blow is conditional.

Distinctive treatment necessary

Each of the five prophecy types deserve distinctive treatment. Mixing the prophecies or merging their respective rules of interpretation renders interpretation impossible. Since we are studying apocalyptic prophecy, we will focus on the rules that apply to this type of prophecy.

1. Apocalyptic prophecy always has a beginning point and ending point in time. Because apocalyptic prophecies have a beginning and ending point in time, they cannot have multiple fulfillments. An apocalyptic sequence can only occur once. Apocalyptic prophecy often contains events within the beginning and ending points

whereby progression towards consummation can be determined. These intermediate events must happen in the order in which they are presented.

2. All prophecies of the Bible are subordinate to apocalyptic structure. This means that apocalyptic prophecy holds greater weight in terms of chronology than non-apocalyptic prophecies. No one prophet has been shown *everything* that God intends to bring about. Each time God speaks to a prophet about the end of time, more detail is provided. By first understanding apocalyptic structure, the visions of the prophets can then be organized chronologically. An apocalyptic prophecy is not fulfilled until all the specifications and the chronology of the prophecy are both met.

3. When a prophecy becomes applicable, the language of the prophecy becomes applicable. For example, John begins Revelation by saying, **"The Revelation of Jesus Christ, which God gave him to show his servants what must soon take place..."** Revelation 1:1 The words "must soon take place" cannot mean 2,000 years. Reason requires that words mean what they say. The point is that when a prophecy

becomes present truth, the language of the prophecy must be taken as literal or analogous unless it is clearly symbolic. If the language is symbolic, the meaning of the symbol must be explained by relevant scripture. Students cannot makeup their own interpretations of symbols. The Bible must interpret itself.

The first point warrants some discussion. As stated before, apocalyptic prophecy is prophecy that lays out a sequence of events. According to rule 1, there are only a few apocalyptic prophecies in the Bible. For example, in Revelation we have the seven seals, seven trumpets and seven last plagues.

It is very important to understand the primacy of apocalyptic structure. For example, the seven trumpets of Revelation are numbered, and follow in consecutive order. If a student demonstrates an interpretation of trumpet 5, that interpretation must recognize the chronological timing of trumpet 4 because trumpet 4 must occur before trumpet 5 does! If we apply rule 2 to the interpretation of trumpet 5, all details regarding trumpets 1-4 must be met too since all aspects of the trumpet prophecy have to be met in order to have a true fulfillment. Since there is only one second coming of Jesus, prophecies having sequences that lead up to that event can only have one fulfillment. Said another way, if trumpets 1 through 5 occur, trumpet 3 can't happen again because trumpet 6 is next sequentially.

Historical applications

Through the centuries, a number of so-called "fulfillments" have been demonstrated from Revelation. The problem with these fulfillments is that they cannot satisfy rule 2 which calls for fulfillment of all details relevant to the prophecy! Since God gives the details to the prophets, a fulfillment can only occur when all the specifications are met. Read Revelation 9:13-21 in your Bible and then read this story:

In the 19th century, Dr. Josiah Litch, a Methodist minister, concluded that trumpets 5 and 6 in Revelation 9 concerned Mohammedanism. He was convinced that the 6th trumpet described in Revelation 9 predicted the fall of the Ottoman Turkish empire. Dr. Litch wrote a book in 1838 titled, "The Probability of the Second Coming of Christ About A.D. 1843" and in it he wrote, "But the duration of their dominion (the Moslems) over the Greek empire... (is) 541 years and 15 days... If the time for commencing the periods was at the time of the first onset of the Ottomans upon the Greeks, July 27, 1299, then the whole period will end in August, 1840." Ibid, page 134. As August, 1840, drew near, Litch predicted the actual date to be August 11.

Casual students of world history are aware of the powerful Ottoman Turkish empire. Those fierce Moslems were undisputed rulers of the middle East for several centuries. But the kingdoms of man come and go. Ottoman glory faded due to a number of humiliating wars. In 1774, Turkey signed a treaty with Christian Russia allowing Russia the right of approval in certain Turkish internal affairs. In 1833 Turkey signed another treaty with Russia which made the ruler of Turkey subject to the Russian tsar. In exchange, Turkey was given protection from Egypt. But in 1839, Egypt seized the Turkish navy as well as a great deal of land. Turkey quickly appealed for help. Four Christian powers (England, Russia, Austria and Prussia) forced a treaty between Turkey and Egypt, and it was signed in London in July of 1840. Egypt released the Turkish navy, reduced the size of its army, withdrew from Syria and resumed paying tribute to Turkey.

On August 11, 1840, Turkey accepted the treaty! Did this fulfill the prophecy of the 6th trumpet? The fact that something of political importance happened on the anticipated day of August 11, 1840 sent shivers among prophetic students of that day. They were convinced that the 6th trumpet had been fulfilled! But was the prophecy fulfilled? Were all details of the prophecy met? A number of problems prevent this conclusion from being regarded as a fulfillment. Four distinct problems stand out:

1. There is no question that the sixth trumpet is a great war. But, this trumpet does not identify which political power rises or falls as a result of the war. Litch thought that the war between Egypt and Turkey qualified but, the Ottoman Empire did not fall or collapse in August of 1840. In fact, Turkey is today a sovereign state.

2. In October of 1582, ten days were eliminated from the calendar to correct the calendar with respect to earth's position with the sun. Dr. Litch did not adjust the timing of his conclusions to compensate, thus the August 11 date is invalid even if we follow his rules or concepts of interpretation.

3. Dr. Litch assumed that the phrase, "an hour, a day, a month and a year" represented a quantity of 391 years, 15 days. He arrived at this conclusion by assuming the phrase was cumulative and then he applied the day/year principle. It is now known that the phrase is translated incorrectly in the KJV. The phrase actually represents a specific moment in time rather than a sum of years. Most translations of the Bible in this century support this corrected understanding.

4. The final and greatest obstacle to Dr. Litch's application is that fulfillment of the first 5 trumpets has not been clearly demonstrated. If we follow the sequence of the seven trumpets, trumpet 6 can only occur after the first five trumpets!

To his credit, Dr. Litch later withdrew his announcement that the 6th trumpet had been fulfilled in August, 1840. He became convinced that what appeared to be a fulfillment, was not a fulfillment. Dr. Litch later concluded, "the trumpets are yet future and will occur shortly before the second coming of Christ."

This story is told to point out a very important issue. Throughout the centuries, people have attempted to explain Revelation's story and show that some piece or part has been fulfilled. However, unless we maintain fidelity to the rules mentioned earlier, we don't have fulfillment! The author believes that even though many have attempted to explain Revelation's story through the centuries, the story belongs exclusively to the last generation. Because they live at the end of time, they alone have this opportunity.

Revelation's timing

In order to appreciate and understand Revelation's story, the student has to determine a place in time where the story begins. Most Bible students assumed the story began with the ascension of Christ (31 A.D.). After all, there are no specific dates mentioned in Revelation.

Remember, there is a demonstrated prophetic mechanism: Prophetic things are understood on or about the time of fulfillment. We will see in the next lesson that Revelation's story has two parts. The first part applies to the seven churches and the second part begins in 1844. For now, you need to know a little more about 1844. This year did not come and go unnoticed.

As the year 1840 approached, people in Europe and America came to understand the importance of the 2,300 days of Daniel 8:14. In America they were known as Millerites or followers of William Miller. Miller, a licensed Baptist minister, set northeastern America astir with his prophetic message that Jesus was returning to earth "about 1844." Miller understood the "cleansing" of the sanctuary to be the cleansing of earth from sin - thus, he concluded, the second coming must occur sometime during 1843 or '44. At the height of his popularity about 100,000 people of various denominations subscribed to his general conclusions that Jesus was about to return!

Miller was not a single voice preaching on the second coming of Jesus. Other great preachers of this era include Charles G. Finney, Dwight L. Moody and Billy Sunday. These and many others contributed to the great spiritual revival of America during the 19th century. Thousands in the eastern half of America gave their lives to the Lord. Camp meetings were held and thousands attended. A large number of Americans were "spiritually revived" and then disappointed.

Because Jesus didn't come (as anticipated), the revival died. Protestant churches in general became disillusioned with prophetic study. General skepticism about prophecy characterized Protestantism for more than a century. Then, in the early 1970's, prophetic interest began to come alive. Suddenly, Hal Lindsey's book, "The Late Great Planet Earth" became a best seller. And today, prophetic study continues to grow into a topic of considerable interest.

So when does Revelation's story begin?

There are two answers to this question. Notice what John is told, **"Write, therefore, what you have seen, what is now and what will take place later."** Revelation 1:19

Just like Daniel's vision (Daniel 8-12), John's vision had information for "his day" and information for "our day." Because some of the information given to the seven churches related to immediate problems, John was clearly told to, **"...write on a scroll what you see and send it to the seven churches: to Ephesus, Smyrna, Pergamum, Thyatira, Sardis, Philadelphia and Laodicea."** Revelation 1:11

The messages to the seven churches initially belonged to them *at the time they were sent to them*. But, in a larger sense, the messages to the seven churches are timeless and universal because the seven churches still exist - not in the same place, nor with the same people. People come and go. Times change, but the seven churches of Jesus remain. The point is that the seven churches represent the body of believers in Christ! The problems with sin haven't changed and the promises and threatenings Jesus gave each church still stand. In fact, Jesus concludes his message to each church saying, **"He who has an ear, let him hear what the Spirit says to the churches."**

The seven churches are not numbered 1 through 7. They are not sequential. They are not apocalyptic. They simultaneously existed in John's day and they simultaneously exist now.

Something old, something new.

We need to observe three things from the messages to the seven churches and see if they apply to ourselves. We need to comprehend the description of Jesus as He is represented to each church; we need to understand the things said to each church and we need to notice the promise given to each church. Notice:

Descriptions of who Jesus is:

1. **Ephesus:** Jesus holds the seven stars in his right hand and walks among the seven lampstands. {1:20-2:1}
2. **Smyrna:** Jesus is the First and Last, who died and came to life again. {2:8}
3. **Pergamum:** Jesus has the sharp, double-edged sword. {2:12}
4. **Thyatira:** Jesus is the Son of God, whose eyes are like blazing fire and whose feet are like burnished bronze. {2:18}
5. **Sardis:** Jesus holds the seven spirits of God and the seven stars. {3:1}
6. **Philadelphia:** Jesus has the key of David. What he shuts - no one can open. What he opens - no one can shut. He sets before us an open door that no one can shut. {3:7,8}
7. **Laodicea:** Jesus is the faithful and true witness, the ruler of God's creation. {3:14}

Timeless warnings or recognition

Notice what Jesus says to each church:

1. **Ephesus:** You have forsaken your first love. {2:4}
2. **Smyrna:** You are afflicted and poor - yet you are rich. Be faithful unto death. {2:9,10}
3. **Pergamum:** You sin by gluttony and sexual immorality Balaam style. (This refers to sins committed with the heathen who don't know any better. Compare with Numbers 22-24.) {2:14}
4. **Thyatira:** You sin by gluttony and sexual immorality Jezebel style. (This refers to sins committed within the church by those knowing better. Compare with I Kings 21 and II Kings 9.) {2:20}
5. **Sardis:** You are dead. Wake up! {3:1,2}
6. **Philadelphia:** You are weak but you are faithful. Hang on. {3:8,10,11}
7. **Laodicea:** You are neither hot nor cold. Repent! {3:15,19}

A promise is a promise

Notice what the victors receive:

1. **Ephesus:** Those overcoming will have the right to eat of the tree of life, which is in the paradise of God. {2:7}
2. **Smyrna:** Those overcoming will not be hurt by the second death. {2:11}
3. **Pergamum:** Those overcoming will receive some of the hidden manna and a white stone with a new name on it. {2:17}
4. **Thyatira:** Those overcoming will have authority over the nations. {2:26}
5. **Sardis:** Those overcoming will be dressed in white and their names will never be erased from the book of life. {3:5}
6. **Philadelphia:** Those overcoming will become a pillar in the temple of God. {3:12}
7. **Laodicea:** Those overcoming will have the right to sit with Jesus on His throne. {3:21}

To the sincere in all churches

Jesus says, **"He who has an ear, let him hear what the Spirit says to the churches."** The messages to the seven churches are timeless. As the number seven denotes fullness or wholeness, the seven churches represent all children of God - scattered over the face of the earth. Which church describes your experience in the Lord? The glory of Jesus is not dimmed by time. Even though He clearly sees the frailty and weakness of His people, He blends encouragement with divine warning. The promised rewards far surpass any price we have to pay. To God be the glory!

Summary

Revelation follows a very careful outline. The story is designed to do two things: First, prepare God's people for the things He is about to do and secondly, provide credibility to the message that God's people will give just before the second coming. The story, the language and the meaning combine in an integral way to reveal the glory of Jesus, hence the book is called, "The Revelation of Jesus."

Rules of interpretation are vitally important. Rules are directly connected to conclusions and good rules are no respecter of persons or denominations.

Revelation had information for the seven churches that existed in John's day, and Revelation contains information for the final and last generation upon earth. The core message to each of the seven churches is still applicable today. Which church do you belong to?

Quiz

1.   What three types of language make up Revelation?

2.   Name three of the five types of prophecy.

3.   Name two of the 3 rules of interpretation.

4.   Which description of Jesus given to the churches do you like best?

5.   In which of the seven churches do you find yourself?

The Seven Seals

Lesson 13

Review

Our last study considered three basic rules of interpretation for apocalyptic prophecies. In shortened form they are:

1. Apocalyptic prophecies have beginning and ending points in time. Events within the prophecy that mark the passage of time must occur in the order in which they are presented.
2. Apocalyptic prophecy is not fulfilled until all the specifications and the chronology of the prophecy are both met.
3. Those elements believed to be symbolic must be interpreted by applicable scripture for the Bible must interpret itself.

We also learned that Revelation has three language types. These are:

1. Symbolic or spiritual
2. Analogue
3. Literal

The student of Revelation must be careful to make the proper distinction between these language types when studying the story.

When does Revelation's story begin?

In order to understand Revelation's story, we must have a chronological beginning date. Because apocalyptic prophecy deals with sequence or structure, a chronological beginning date is extremely important. We saw this point confirmed in our study on Daniel 8. The decree to restore and rebuild Jerusalem in 457 B.C. marked the beginning of the 490 years as well as the 2,300 year prophecy!

We have learned that John's vision (like Daniel's) contained information for his day and information on things that would occur later. How much later? From the outline in the previous lesson, we know that Revelation 4-6 contains a new sequence. These chapters tell us about a great convocation in heaven where Jesus is found worthy to take a book sealed with seven seals. Upon receiving the book, Jesus begins to open the book by breaking one seal open at a time. What is this book? What is inside it? Why is it sealed up? When does this scene take place?

The all important book

We need to read the story that surrounds the book with seven seals. Notice John's remarks:

"After this I looked, and there before me was a door standing open in heaven. And the voice I had first heard speaking to me like a trumpet said, 'Come up here, and I will show you what must take place after this.' {2} At once I was in the Spirit, and there before me was a throne in heaven with someone sitting on it. {3} And the one who sat there had the appearance of jasper and carnelian. A rainbow, resembling an emerald, encircled the throne.

{4} Surrounding the throne were twenty-four other thrones, and seated on them were twenty-four elders. They were dressed in white and had crowns of gold on their heads. {5} From the throne came flashes of lightning, rumblings and peals of thunder. Before the throne, seven lamps were blazing. These are the seven spirits of God.

{6} Also before the throne there was what looked like a sea of glass, clear as crystal. In the center, around the throne, were four living creatures, and they were covered with eyes, in front and in back. {7} The first living creature was like a lion, the second was like an ox, the third had a face like a man, the fourth was like a flying eagle. {8} Each of the four living creatures had six wings and was covered with eyes all around, even under his wings. Day and night they never stop saying: 'Holy, holy, holy is the Lord God Almighty, who was, and is, and is to come.' {9} Whenever the living creatures give glory, honor and thanks to him who sits on the throne and who lives for ever and ever, {10} the twenty-four elders fall down before him who sits on the throne, and worship him who lives for ever and ever. They lay their crowns before the throne and say: {11} 'You are worthy, our Lord and God, to receive glory and honor and power, for you created all things, and by your will they were created and have their being.'

{5:1} Then I saw in the right hand of him who sat on the throne a scroll with writing on both sides and sealed with seven seals. {2} And I saw a mighty angel proclaiming in a loud voice, 'Who is worthy to break the seals and open the scroll?' {3} But no one in heaven or on earth or under the earth could open the scroll or even look inside it.

{4} I wept and wept because no one was found who was worthy to open the scroll or look inside. {5} Then one of the elders said to me, 'Do not weep! See, the Lion of the tribe of Judah, the Root of David, has triumphed. He is able to open the scroll and its seven seals.' {6} Then I saw a Lamb, looking as if it had been slain, standing in the center of the throne, encircled by the four living creatures and the elders. He had seven horns and seven eyes, which are the seven spirits of God sent out into all the earth.

{7} He came and took the scroll from the right hand of him who sat on the throne. {8} And when he had taken it, the four living creatures and the twenty-four elders fell down before the Lamb. Each one had a harp and they were holding golden bowls full of incense, which are the prayers of the saints. {9} And they sang a new song: 'You are worthy to take the scroll and to open its seals, because you were slain, and with your blood you purchased men for God from every tribe and language and people and nation. {10} You have made them to be a kingdom and priests to serve our God, and they will reign on the earth.'

{11} Then I looked and heard the voice of many angels, numbering thousands upon thousands, and ten thousand times ten thousand. They encircled the throne and the living creatures and the elders. {12} In a loud voice they sang: 'Worthy is the Lamb, who was slain, to receive power and wealth and wisdom and strength and honor and glory and praise!' {13} Then I heard every creature in heaven and on earth and under the earth and on the sea, and all that is in them, singing: 'To him who sits on the throne and to the Lamb be praise and honor and glory and power, for ever and ever!' "   Revelation 4 and 5

The elders?

Who are the 24 elders? The Bible doesn't explain who they are in clear terms. They are mentioned 12 times in Revelation. However, there are some very strong clues that reveal their identity. First, the term elder means "one who has gone before," or someone of greater experience. Revelation 5:9 indicates that the elders have been redeemed by the blood of Jesus. Paul tells us that Jesus took some resurrected people to heaven with him at the time of His ascension. Ephesians 4:7,8. But perhaps the greatest evidence supporting the idea that these are people who once lived on earth is the location of their thrones. Understand that billions of angels are in this assembly. The judgment of human beings is taking place. And who should be given a front row seat to observe the fairness and mercy of Jesus? Those who have been redeemed!

The Lamb's book

John clearly saw the Lamb deemed worthy to take this all important book from the right hand of the Father. Revelation 5:7 Even though John does not call the book sealed with seven seals the "book of life" in chapter 5, he clearly refers to this book as the Lamb's book of life in other places in Revelation. It's the only book the Lamb receives in Revelation's story! Notice:

"All inhabitants of the earth will worship the beast - all whose names have not been written in the book of life belonging to the Lamb..." Revelation 13:8

"...The inhabitants of the earth whose names have not been written in the book of life from the creation of the world will be astonished when they see the beast..." Revelation 17:8 (Note when the book of life was written.)

"Nothing impure will ever enter it (New Jerusalem), nor will anyone who does what is shameful or deceitful, but only those whose names are written in the Lamb's book of life." Revelation 21:27

Daniel knew of this book even though he does not call it by name! Speaking about the close of probation, Daniel says, **"At that time Michael, the great prince who protects your people, will arise. There will be a time of distress such as has not happened from the beginning of nations until then. But at that time your people - everyone whose name is found written in the book - will be delivered."** Daniel 12:1

King David knew of this book. **"Your eyes saw my unformed body. All the days ordained for me were written in your book before one of them came to be."** Psalm 139:16

There is only one place in the Bible that tells us when this book is opened: it's at the end of the 1,000 years. This is when the 7th seal is broken. John says, **"And I saw the dead, great and small, standing before the throne, and books were opened. Another book was opened, which is the book of life..."** Revelation 20:12

The book of life was composed and perfectly sealed up before the creation of the world. It contains the story of the plan of salvation and the outcome. When the great day of reckoning comes at the end of the thousand years, the resurrection of the wicked takes place. Revelation 20:5 At this one and only time in earth's existence, all members of the human race are alive! It's a grand and terrible moment.

With the wicked resurrected, Satan immediately stirs the vast multitude with rebellion. He convinces the numberless crowd that God intends to do them harm. He incites a dramatic uprising to destroy the New Jerusalem and the saints. As the wicked rush upon the city, Jesus speaks. The multitude is stopped in their tracks.

Silence falls upon the breathless mob for about half an hour. Revelation 8:1 Jesus, as King of Kings and Lord of Lords, speaks. The anger and rebellion of the numberless mob dissipates. As lightning pierces the darkness, the wicked realize they stand before their Maker. He is not a tyrant. He is not angry. He speaks.

Jesus explains the plan of salvation to the multitude. The wicked behold the love of God. Each person understands the economy of salvation. Each person's life is presented from the open books. The wicked see their deeds just as God saw their deeds. Each person beholds the spiritual influences of good and evil upon their life. They see the choices which were made. He who sees the hearts and reads the motives reveals sin to them with unvarnished clarity. The wicked know why they are condemned. All justification for sin is expelled in the light of God's love. With every motive fully exposed, sin is seen as nothing more than love for self. The wicked now know what the love of Jesus is, why he died on Calvary and why they cannot be saved.

At the end of this revelation, every knee bows before Jesus with deepest emotion. The wicked admit Jesus is fair and just in his eternal decision and the righteous admit that Jesus is unbelievably merciful. Jesus said, **"...before me every knee will bow; by me every tongue will swear. They will say of me 'In the Lord alone are righteousness and strength' All who have raged against him will come to him and be put to shame. But in the Lord all the descendants of Israel will be found righteous and will exult."** Isaiah 45:23-25 Even though the wicked admit the justice and love of God, they can not change their evil course. Outside of God there is no power to overcome sin! Such is the heinous power of sin.

John says, **"Then another book was opened which is the book of life."** At last, the breaking of the 7th seal allows the mysterious book of life to be opened. Heaven's most intriguing book has been sealed for thousands of years and it contains not only the story of salvation, but the names of all who have been granted eternal life! The victors stand around the throne with deep interest.

What a moment! What a day! If the number of the redeemed of all ages is 14,567,259,123,382 that's the exact number of names remaining there! The names of the wicked were blotted out when the book was written. Both the wicked and the righteous watch with amazement. The wicked have no argument with the salvation of the saints. The mercy and justice of Jesus has been revealed to them. The righteous bow in awe that Jesus knew them by name before the world existed! Consider the significance of this moment. One group bows before Jesus recognizing his fairness and justice while the other group bows before Jesus recognizing his love and mercy!

The opening of this book proves two very important things. First, it unquestionably proves the omniscience of God. He knows everything about everything. The contents of the book, written before the world came into existence, clearly describes what actually took place upon earth. Each member of the human family beholds the story written in the book of life, and knows the story is accurate for he was an actor in the story. The book of life is identical to the book of deeds with one exception. The names of the wicked are blotted out of the book of life.

Secondly, the book of life unquestionably proves that God actually granted the power of choice to each person. Each member of the human family knows that his eternal reward was his choice. Those inside the New Jerusalem know they are only there because they chose Jesus as their Saviour. Those outside the city know they are there because they chose to reject the promptings of the Holy Spirit. The net effect is this: Even though God knows everything about everything, He does not manipulate his subjects on the basis of foreknowledge. The power of choice was freely bestowed upon all his children and the opening of this book confirms it!

The book of life is so-called because it contains the names of those who will live forever. This book will be studied for eternity. The contents of this book will be compared with the Bible and the books of record throughout the ages, for the redeemed will never cease to marvel at the love of God.

One last and very important point. The greatest punishment God gives a human being is the "reality of forfeiture." When the wicked behold with their own eyes what they *chose* to forfeit, words will not be able to describe their anguish. The wicked, in deepest grief, turn and vent their remorse upon each other. They begin to kill one another and to finish the carnage, Jesus sends fire from heaven and burns them up. Sin and sinners are no more. The universe is free at last! Free of sin.

Back to the book with seven seals

So, when does Jesus take the book sealed with seven seals? There are only three choices for the answer to this question.

a.   Shortly after his ascension

b.   1844

c.   Sometime in the future

The Bible answers the question! In fact, Daniel provides the key. Notice Daniel's vision recorded in Daniel 7:

"As I looked, thrones were set in place, and the Ancient of Days took His seat. His clothing was as white as snow; the hair of His head was white like wool. His throne was flaming with fire, and its wheels were all ablaze. A river of fire was flowing, coming out from before Him. Thousands upon thousands attended him; ten thousand times ten thousand stood before Him. The court was seated, and the books were opened... and there before me was one like a son of man, coming with the clouds of heaven. He approached the Ancient of Days and was led into His presence. He was given authority, glory and sovereign power; all peoples, na-tions and men of every language worshiped him. His dominion is an everlasting dominion that will not pass away, and His kingdom is one that will never be destroyed." Daniel 7:9-14

Consider the parallels

Several parallels immediately appear between Daniel 7 and Revelation 4 and 5. The most important parallel in these two scenes is that Jesus is especially honored. He receives authority, glory and sovereign power at a specific ceremony in both cases. According to Daniel, this point in time is directly connected to the court room scene. According to John, this point in time is connected with a Lamb receiving the book of life. It is unreasonable to suggest that Jesus receives glory, sovereign power and authority on *two* separate occasions. In other words, Jesus wouldn't need sovereign power con-ferred upon Him again if it had been previously given to him.

Daniel and John favorably compare:

Dan 7:9 and Rev 4:2,4

I looked, thrones were set in place.

Before me was a throne with 24 thrones surrounding it oc-cupied by 24 elders.

Dan 7:9 and Rev 4:3,4

The Ancient of Days took His seat. His clothing was as white as snow, the hair of His head was white like wool.

The One who sat there had the appearance of a jasper and (the brilliance of a ruby). The elders were dressed in white.

Dan 7:9,10 and Rev 4:5

His throne was flaming with fire and its wheels were all ablaze. And the books were opened.

From the throne came flashes of lightning, rumblings and peals of thunder. Before the throne seven lamps were blazing.

Dan 7:13 and Rev 5:7

I saw one like "a son of man." He approached the Ancient of Days.

The Lamb approached the Father sitting on the throne and took the scroll from His right hand.

Dan 7:14 and Rev 5:9,12

He was given authority, glory and sovereign power.

The Elders sing of Jesus, **"You are worthy to take the scroll and open its seals."** Billions of angels sing, **"Worthy is the Lamb, who was slain, to receive power and wealth and wisdom and strength and honor and glory and praise!"**

The parallel between the scenes is unmistakable. Daniel and John saw the same heavenly court room scene. Daniel saw a human being, "a son of man", approach the Father sitting on His throne and John saw "a Lamb looking as though it had been slain" come before the Father as He sat upon His throne. Daniel saw thrones put in place and the court convene with billions of angels in attendance. He saw the Father take His seat and the books of records were opened. He saw Jesus approach the Father and receive sovereign power and glory.

John also saw a great convocation in the throne room of the universe and specifically mentions seeing 24 thrones around the Father's throne. Billions of angels were in attendance. Heaven's most important book was in the right hand of the Father. A search through the universe was conducted for someone worthy to receive this most important book - for some heavenly process cannot continue until *this book* is received. John wept because the business of heaven was suspended until someone was found worthy to receive the book of life. After an intensive investigation throughout the universe, Jesus was *judged* worthy to receive the book. The elders along with billions of angels sang enthusiastically as power, wealth, honor and praise were conferred upon Jesus.

Jesus received book of life in 1844

After comparing the two visions, there is no question that Daniel and John saw *the recognition and promotion given to Jesus when He received power, wealth, strength, wisdom and praise.* From Daniel we learn that Jesus is promoted at the time heaven's court convenes in 1844. From John we learn that Jesus is promoted at the time He receives the book sealed with seven seals. The honor conferred upon Jesus in these scenes confirms that John and Daniel saw the same scene. Thus the book of life was given to Jesus in 1844.

Two other matters confirm 1844 as the correct date. First, on the Old Testament Day of Atonement, the High Priest had to be found worthy to officiate on behalf of Israel before he could conduct the service. (See Leviticus 16) If we understand that the courtroom scene described by Daniel and John symbolizes the actual Day of Atonement in the heavenly sanctuary, it is appropriate that Jesus is found worthy to conduct the services related to this occasion.

The last point confirming 1844 as the date when Jesus received the book sealed with seven seals comes from the internal harmony of Revelation's story. Since the story has not been studied yet, this point is not helpful at this moment to the student. However, as we study Revelation, the harmony of the sum of the parts will continue to confirm the importance and significance of 1844. When we look into the various sequences that involve timing, the significance of this point will be clearly realized.

What are the seven seals?

According to Webster, a seal is a device that secures an object. In this case, 7 seals perfectly secures the contents of the book of life. This means no one can get into the book and change its contents. What was written down in the book cannot be altered. In fact, the content of the book of life is not revealed in Revelation's story. The contents are not revealed until every person who ever lived stands before Jesus! John saw *when* the book was opened (Revelation 20:12), but he did not see *what* was in the book.

The opening of the seals implies two things. First, as each seal opens, the contents of the book are chronologically nearer to exposure. The seals are numbered consecutively, thus when the 4th seal is opened, the events that occur under this seal confirm where in the sequence we are. When the 6th seal is opened, the second coming of

Jesus occurs - but keep in mind, the book still has one more seal to be opened. The book is not opened at the second coming.

Secondly, and more importantly, the opening of the seals only have meaning when we understand their relationship to the book. *What point is made unsealing the book of seven seals if the exposure of the contents of the book is not the object of the sequence?* The seals progress in a definite sequence towards the climactic moment when the book of life is opened. The progression of the seals is viewed in heaven by billions of attending angels (remember, they haven't seen inside the book) and on earth by people studying Revelation's story! These things may not be easy to understand at first, but those who study will understand. Daniel was told, **"None of the wicked will understand, but those who are wise will understand."** Daniel 12:10

A very brief review of the 7 seals is outlined below:

1. Rider on white horse - sets out to conquer.
2. Rider on red horse - causes conflict and war.
3. Rider on black horse - warns of judgment.
4. Rider on pale horse - brings devastation.
5. Martyrs for truth's sake.
6. The Lamb's second coming.
7. Silence for about a half hour.

Jesus received the book of life in 1844 and began opening the seals at that time. We will see that the first three seals were opened during a short period of time and that these seals prepare the world for the events described in the next three seals!

Before we examine the seals, we must understand an important point that is often overlooked. John is in vision and he has been taken to the heavenly throne room to view things that occur at the appointed time of the end. In other words, John was zoomed forward in time to behold events that occur at the end of the world. Remember John was told, "write the things you have seen, what is now and what will take place later." Revelation 4 begins an apocalyptic sequence that begins with 1844 and ends at the end of the millennium.

The four horses

The four horses of Revelation are not unique to Revelation. Zechariah saw four horses having the same colors! Zechariah was told the four horses represent the four spirits of heaven that stand in the presence of the Lord of the whole world. Zechariah 6:5 These go throughout the earth at God's command to accomplish His will. Zechariah 1:10,11 Zechariah saw the black horse go north, the white horse went west, the pale or dappled horse went south and the red horse, by inference, went east. Zechariah 6:6 These four horses go throughout the whole world. These four horses symbolize the four living creatures that stand in the presence of God. These four living creatures might be thought of as "senior angels" having great responsibilities. They are appointed to carry out special services throughout the universe of God. These angels insure that God's desires are carried out. (For more detailed study on these four creatures and their responsibilities read Ezekiel 1 & 10.)

The seals begin

Each horse and rider represent the works or actions of the four living creatures. As Jesus opens each seal, He commissions a specific process that leads to the conclusion of the plan of salvation. Very important point: the effect and influence of the seals is both cumulative and associative. This means that the conquering begun in seal one is concluded in seal six. The process begun in seal two reaches its climax during seal five and the understanding of seal three prepares some "teachers" for the events that transpire during seal four. (See diagram at end of this chapter.)

In other words, a seal doesn't begin and end so that the next seal can begin and end. Rather, the first three seals begin certain processes

which remain in motion until their counterpart concludes their work. It was for this very reason that Jesus was given sovereign power! He starts three processes upon earth that He must personally manage. Even more, He must manage the outcome of each process so that the gospel accomplishes its task. Just as the rider of each horse controls the action of the horse, Jesus sends the four living creatures to earth with special assignments. As each "senior angel" prepares to do his work, John is invited to observe. They each say to John, "Come."

First seal

"I watched as the Lamb opened the first of the seven seals. Then I heard one of the four living creatures say in a voice like thunder, 'Come!' I looked, and there before me was a white horse! Its rider held a bow, and he was given a crown, and he rode out as a conqueror bent on conquest." Revelation 6:1,2

The first horse and rider (senior angel) goes out of the heavenly sanctuary to conquer something on earth. Nothing is conquered in the first seal. No special event in heaven or on earth marks the opening of this seal. Rather, this seal marks the beginning conquest of Jesus. In 1844, Jesus our High Priest, set out to conclude the sin problem by revealing more truth about the everlasting gospel. Time has come to put the everlasting gospel in final form, for soon, it must go to every person on earth.

The great revival in Protestant North America in the early 19th century prepared the way for understanding the arrival of 1844. The work that began under this seal sets the stage for the final presentation of the gospel. The entire world must hear the full gospel! John saw the consummating victory of the gospel. He saw the victory of the 144,000 and a great multitude which no man could number. He says, **"And I saw what looked like a sea of glass mixed with fire and, standing beside the sea, those who had been victorious over the beast and his image and over the number of his name..."** Revelation 15:2

Second seal

"When the Lamb opened the second seal, I heard the second living creature say, 'Come!' Then another horse came out, a fiery red one. Its rider was given power to take peace from the earth and to make men slay each other. To him was given a large sword." Revelation 6:3,4

The second horse (senior angel) goes out of the heavenly sanctuary with a large sword. This sword eventually causes men to slay each other. A number of Bible students are reluctant to identify this event as having a heavenly origin. But Jesus told his disciples, **"Do not suppose that I have come to bring peace to the earth. I did not come to bring peace, but a sword."** Matthew 10:34 The sword of Jesus is the power of truth. Hebrews 4:12 says, **"The word of God is living and active. Sharper than any double-edged sword..."** Paul said, **"Take the helmet of salvation and the sword of the Spirit, which is the word of God."** Ephesians 6:17 In Revelation 2:12, John describes Jesus to the church in Pergamum as, **"Him who has the sharp, double-edged sword."** Jesus said to this church, **"Repent therefore! Otherwise, I will soon come to you and will fight against them with the sword of my mouth."** Revelation 2:16

We will study the war and bloodshed that occurs all over the earth in lessons 18 and 19 as a result of the work done by this senior angel. The coming war will be a contest between truth and falsehood. This seal points forward to a time when people will kill one another over truth! Here is a subtle but very important point. Notice that the text describing the second seal does not have to mean that the slaying occurs *at the time* the second seal is opened. (Neither is the conquering described in the first seal accomplished during the time of the first seal.) Rather, the consequence of the second seal is seen *when peace is taken from the earth and men slay each other* on account of the sword!

What is the sword? Allowing the Bible to interpret itself, we must conclude from the texts above that the sword represents the "Word of God."

Can we look back to the time period following 1844 and find anything to mark the opening of this seal? Yes! The formation of Bible societies during the mid to late 19th century by Protestants fulfills the meaning of this seal! Remember, the gospel commission belongs to them after 1798. The translation and distribution of the Bible into every nation on earth has grown immensely since 1844. In those days a large number of Protestant churches in Europe and North America formed Bible and Missionary Societies to carry the gospel to all the world! The late 19th century marks a "high-water mark" for the establishment and activity of mission service by Protestant denominations. People gave liberally to the printing and distribution of the Bible. In fact, no book on earth has ever been translated and distributed to the extent the Bible has. No other book on earth has overcome the popularity of the Bible and the Bible will be the book upon which the coming great controversy will be focused!

Third seal

"When the Lamb opened the third seal, I heard the third living creature say, 'Come!' I looked, and there before me was a black horse! Its rider was holding a pair of scales in his hand. Then I heard what sounded like a voice among the four living creatures, saying, 'A quart of wheat for a day's wages, and three quarts of barley for a day's wages, and do not damage the oil and the wine!' " Revelation 6:5,6

The third horse (senior angel) goes out of the heavenly sanctuary with a pair of scales and a message. The scales imply a judgment or decision making process. We know from Daniel that the books of record were opened in 1844 and that Jesus began an investigation of the records of the dead. The work of the third senior angel is to see that people on earth become aware of what Jesus is doing in the heavenly sanctuary. During the past 146 years, the understanding and awareness of the investigative judgment has grown around the world. Even though general knowledge of the ongoing judgment process is not yet widespread among the population of the earth, several million people already know about it! Those who understand this truth will soon be in a position to explain the even more important judgment process that is coming: the judgment of the living!

The message that accompanies this seal is twofold. First, wages are promised to those who will help spread this special message and secondly, a warning is given to those who should hear it. Even though many years have passed since the judgment hour message first began, and those who first preached the judgment hour message are now dead, all who have helped to carry this message throughout the earth will receive their due reward!

The warning portion of this message counsels those who hear the judgment hour message not to reject the understanding of 1844. Oil symbolizes the Holy Spirit (Zechariah 4), and wine symbolizes doctrine or teachings (Revelation 17:2). The admonition "don't harm the oil or the wine" apparently means "receive the Holy Spirit and the truth concerning the ministry of Jesus in the heavenly sanctuary." (For an Old Testament parallel on the use of wheat, barley, wine and oil as wages, see II Chronicles 2:10-15.)

First three seals set global stage for next three seals

These three seals have been opened. As each seal opened, there is a progressive revelation of Jesus in heaven and on earth. Who Jesus is, what He is and how He intends to conclude the gospel commission becomes clearer to the watching angels and to a growing number of people on earth. Truth is ever progressive and the seals demonstrate just that. The first three seals were opened over a short time period beginning in 1844. By 1864, the judgment hour message was understood well enough to be proclaimed abroad! And for more than a century, the activities described in these three seals have influenced the earth, in effect, setting the stage for what is about to happen!!!

Fourth seal

"When the Lamb opened the fourth seal, I heard the voice of the fourth living creature say, 'Come!' I looked, and there before me was a pale horse! Its rider was named Death, and Hades was following close behind him. They were given power over a fourth of the earth to kill by sword, famine and plague, and by the wild beasts of the earth." Revelation 6:7,8

The opening of the fourth seal brings global devastation. This senior angel is the angel of death. Perhaps this is the same angel that flew over Egypt and killed the firstborn children and animals of the Egyptians. Exodus 12-13 Perhaps he is also the same angel that killed 185,000 of Sennacherib's army. II Kings 19 Regardless of his identity, his influence upon the earth is unmistakeable.

Jesus sends this senior angel to earth with four terrible judgments to arrest the attention of the world. These judgments are identified as: sword, famine, plague and wild beasts. 25% of the earth will perish in these judgments! For deeper study on these four dreadful judgments, you must read Ezekiel 14:12-23.

The fourth seal is the next one to open. This is self-evident. From the perspective of chronological timing alone, the devastating results of this seal have not been observed upon earth since the seals began opening in 1844. We will also see that the events during this seal are a great catalyst marking the beginning of the judgment of the living! The death and destruction attending the 4th seal is fully explained in Revelation's story on the seven trumpets and seven last plagues. These will be studied in considerable detail in future lessons.

One last point. The first four seals are actions carried out by senior angels (the four living creatures). The fifth seal is carried out by the followers of Jesus on earth, and the sixth seal is carried out by Jesus Himself!

Fifth seal

"When he opened the fifth seal, I saw under the altar the souls of those who had been slain because of the word of God and the testimony they had maintained. They called out in a loud voice, 'How long, Sovereign Lord, holy and true, until you judge the inhabitants of the earth and avenge our blood?' Then each of them was given a white robe, and they were told to wait a little longer, until the number of their fellow servants and brothers who were to be killed as they had been was completed." Revelation 6:9-11

The opening of the fifth seal ushers in a period of martyrdom. Why would Jesus allow martyrdom to come upon His people? There are two reasons. First, persecution separates pretense from substance. When the price for being a Christian is great, who will be willing to bear the cross and follow the teachings of Jesus? The pure in heart that love God's truth.

In America, the cost of being a Christian has been for the most part, easy. We have religious liberty. We can worship without intimidation or fear. We have freedom of speech. We can teach and believe whatever we want. We are truly blessed! But this blessing has brought a curse. We have become lazy, weak and in many instances, corrupt. Christianity today is comprised of many fair-weather Christians filled with external piety. Protestant America has become degenerate and looks more like a hospital for sin-sick people than an army of soldiers prepared for the final conflict with Satan!

The second reason the 5th seal brings martyrdom is that when the 5th seal is opened, Satan is personally upon earth claiming to be God. Those following Jesus will recognize the devil for what he is and will do everything possible to tell the world of his supreme deceptions. Think of it! With much of the world receiving the evil impostor as God, those who fearlessly identify the imposter as the devil will not be looked upon favorably! How would you feel if someone called your God "the devil?" If ever there was a holy war, this will be it. Those killing the followers of Jesus (who remains in heaven until the sixth seal is opened) will actually be told by the evil imposter they are doing God a service!

Sixth seal

"I watched as he opened the sixth seal. There was a great earthquake. The sun turned black like sackcloth made of goat hair, the whole moon turned blood red, {13} and the stars in the sky fell to earth, as late figs drop from a fig tree when shaken by a strong wind. {14} The sky receded like a scroll, rolling up, and every mountain and island was removed from its place. {15} Then the kings of the earth, the princes, the generals, the rich, the mighty, and every slave and every free man hid in caves and among the rocks of the mountains. {16} They called to the mountains and the rocks, 'Fall on us and hide us from the face of him who sits on the throne and from the wrath of the Lamb! {17} For the great day of their wrath has come, and who can stand?'"** Revelation 6:12-17

The opening of the sixth seal brings Jesus to the rescue of His people. The opening of the sixth seal is the second coming. John describes King Jesus as riding on the white horse, having the title, "King of kings and Lord of Lords" upon His sash. Revelation 19:11-16

Just as the work of the first seal began on a white horse in 1844, so the work of the sixth seal is concluded on a white horse. Jesus set out to conquer in 1844 and at the second coming, he conquers! John says, **"I saw heaven standing open and there before me was a white horse, whose rider is called Faithful and True. With justice he judges and makes war... Out of his mouth comes a sharp sword with which to strike down the nations. He will rule them with an iron scepter...' "** Revelation 19:11,15

Seventh seal

"When he opened the seventh seal, there was silence in heaven

for about half an hour." Revelation 8:1

The opening of the seventh seal occurs at the end of the 1,000 years and the story within the book of life - now unsealed - is fully exposed. The importance of this seal will be seen again in later lessons.

SUMMARY

The first three seals prepare the world stage for the development of the next three seals. The relationships within the seals becomes apparent when compared to their counterpart. The breaking open of each seal reveals a new dimension in the work of Jesus as our High Priest in the heavenly sanctuary!

The opening of each seal moves us chronologically towards the second coming and the great day of reckoning at the end of the 1000 years. In the next lesson, we will study the consequences of the seals in more detail. You will see how the opening of the 4th seal marks the beginning of the judgment of the living! Review this lesson carefully for those who study Bible prophecy study the deep things of God.

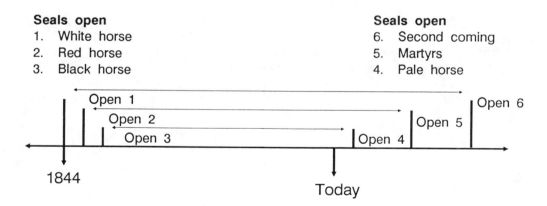

Seals open
1. White horse
2. Red horse
3. Black horse

Seals open
6. Second coming
5. Martyrs
4. Pale horse

The first three seals mark the beginning of three processes that prepare the world for the next three seals. As each seal is opened, Jesus and His everlasting gospel are more clearly revealed.

The First Six Seals

Quiz

1. Do you think John and Daniel saw the same scene that occurred in 1844?

2. When did Jesus receive the book sealed with 7 seals?

3. What is in the book sealed with seven seals?

4. What is proven when the book of life is finally opened?

5. Which seals have been opened?

Notes:

The Seven Trumpets Part I

Lesson 14

Review

Our previous study focused on the seven seals. Because the seals are chronological in nature, it is critically important that we establish when the seals begin to be opened if we are to identify their relationship to time. In our last lesson, we saw how Daniel and Revelation harmoniously combine and bring us to the conclusion that 1844 is the year that Jesus received the book sealed with seven seals. The harmony of the sum of prophetic parts brings encouragement and enlightenment to students of prophecy! Even more, we shall see in this lesson that Revelation's sequences internally harmonize with 1844.

The issue of the worthiness of Jesus as our High Priest also brings us to 1844. Remember, in the Old Testament, the High Priest had to be found worthy and his sacrifice accepted *before* he could officiate on behalf of Israel! Leviticus 16

The previous lesson also suggested that three seals were opened within a short time period following 1844. As every drama requires a stage, the first three seals prepare the earth for the next three seals. In addition, there is historical evidence supporting the interpretation given to the first three seals. The cumulative influence of the first three seals has been steadily growing. We will discover in this lesson just how well the senior angels of the first three seals have been at their work!

The fourth seal

Carefully review the fourth seal: **"When the Lamb opened the fourth seal, I heard the voice of the fourth living creature say, 'Come!' I looked, and there before me was a pale horse! Its rider was named Death, and Hades was following close behind him. They were given power over a fourth of the earth to kill by**

sword, famine and plague, and by the wild beasts of the earth." Revelation 6:7,8

The strongest internal evidence that the fourth seal is the next one to be opened is that the devastation described in this seal has not yet occurred. The fourth seal indicates that 25% of the earth will be destroyed by these four dreadful judgments. Why will Jesus open the fourth seal and send these four terrible judgments throughout the earth?

An angry God?

There is much confusion about the character of God in the world today. By misrepresenting the character of God, the devil has lead many people to either hate or ignore God. Even worse, the devil has lead most of the Protestant world to regard Jesus much like a heavenly Santa Clause. By over- emphasizing the great compassion and mercy of Jesus, and diminishing the legitimacy of God's commandments, many are ignorant of the teachings of Jesus that require obedience. As the bumper sticker says, "Jesus is either Lord over all or He's not Lord at all!"

Think about your own character for a moment. Have you ever had someone misrepresent you before people that didn't know you? Even worse, has someone spread lies about you among those who knew you? How hard is it to overcome slanderous falsehoods?

The Bible declares that God is love. Divine love is the balance between justice and mercy. Jesus is all-merciful, and yet, He requires justice. He wants people to live as He lives. The prophet Micah wrote, **"He has showed you, O man, what is good. And what does the Lord require of you? To act justly and to love mercy and to walk humbly with your God."** Micah 6:8

The Bible tells us that Jesus is very capable of anger, and in times past, his wrath has broken out upon individuals, cities, nations and even the world! Review these four stories in your Bible that demonstrate the wrath of Jesus:

1. Individuals: Korah, Dathan and Abiram (Numbers 16)
2. Cities: Sodom and Gomorrah (Genesis 19)
3. Nations: The Philistines (Joshua 5:13-6:27)
4. Earth: The Flood (Genesis 6,7)

Each of these stories bring out a very important truth. Jesus rises up in anger and wrath when His mercy and patience no longer has a redeeming effect.

The truth hurts

Satan is delighted when people believe that salvation comes by assumption. Many popular preachers and evangelists preach "Christ without the cross" and consequently become popular. They excite multitudes with stories of powerful miracles. They proclaim ecstatic messages about the power of Jesus and talk extensively about healing from sickness. But few clearly define sin and say that we can and must obtain victory over it. People don't like to have their sins pointed out! Think about it. If Jesus were alive upon the earth today, His teachings would meet with the same rejection as when He walked upon the earth. When it comes to sin, the truth hurts today just like it hurt when He walked upon the earth.

The problem is that we human beings have a hard time seeing our own faults. Without a clear definition of sin we can't appreciate or understand the malignancy of sin. By watering down the high standard of righteousness, Satan has led this nation (and all the others) into greater sin. Consequently, problems without solutions escalate.

We cannot appreciate the salvation of Jesus without an understanding of the offensiveness and power of sin. Until we comprehend some of the magnitude of sin, we cannot appreciate the meaning of "being saved." Until we admit our helplessness to overcome sin, we cannot appreciate the transforming power of Jesus nor can we realize our desperate need for His great love. Satan has cleverly worked through the large religious systems of the world to disguise sin. In general, people don't understand what sin is, nor do they know how to obtain victory over it! But the everlasting gospel has the answer! This is another reason why the gospel must go to the world. It must expose the religious systems of the world for what they are!

The devil has encompassed the 7 great religious systems in the world so that they serve his purposes. In very general terms, the premise of each system is:

1. **Atheism:** This system teaches there is no God. Man is supreme.
2. **Heathenism:** This system is ignorant of the living God and creates its own god(s) as needed.
3. **Eastern Mysticism:** This system teaches that man is immortal and can become God.
4. **Judaism:** This system teaches that man is saved by obedience to the laws of God.
5. **Islam:** This system teaches that man is saved through obedience to the teachings of Mohammed.

6. **Catholicism:** This system teaches that man is saved through obedience to the teachings of the church.

7. **Protestantism:** This system teaches that man is saved by believing that he is saved.

As you look at these seven systems, you'll notice they neatly fit into one of three categories:

1. There is no salvation, for there is no God.

2. Man saves himself through obedience.

3. Man is saved by assuming he is saved.

The world's 7 religious systems are built on false assumptions. (This is not saying that God does not have sincere people within each system. Those living up to all they know to be right are claimed by God as his children. Review lessons 5 and 6.) But falsehoods, once assumed or accepted, lead people away from God's truth and ultimately, people do terrible things in the name of God. Jesus warned his disciples, **"They will put you out of the synagogue; in fact, a time is coming when anyone who kills you will think he is offering a service to God. They will do such things because they have not know the Father or me."** John 16:2,3

Back to the fourth seal

Jesus has prepared a final test for the world to find out who loves Him *and* His truth. The test is carefully made to test our love for principles of righteousness. It will not be enough to be sincere and dedicated when the test is applied. Hitler was sincere and dedicated to his terrible ideas and the world suffered at his hands. Sincerity is not the most important element in life. The most important point is TRUTH. Who loves and seeks for more of God's Truth? Who lives up to all the truth he knows? Who loves the truth of God so much that he would be willing to suffer or die for its sake?

John saw the saints struggling to defend truth at the end of the world. He says, **"Then the dragon was enraged at the woman and went off to make war against the rest of her offspring - those who obey God's commandments and hold to the testimony of Jesus."** Revelation 12:17 As he watched, John saw the martyrdom of the saints that occurs during the fifth seal and John was told, **"This calls for patient endurance on the part of the saints who obey God's commandments and remain faithful to Jesus."** Revelation 14:12

In 1844, Jesus began judging the dead. Their deeds and actions are recorded in the books of record. But how does Jesus judge the living? Their lives are still being lived out.

They continue to make choices. Because the world is so diverse with languages, cultures and religious beliefs, God has designed the judgment of the living in such a way that the living will choose their own eternal destiny. As each person makes his decision about the gospel, Jesus eternally seals them in it! Here's a brief scenario:

Jesus sends His four dreadful judgments to awaken and arouse the earth to the sinfulness of its course. These four judgments (also described in Ezekiel 14) arrest the indifference of the people of earth to the gospel so they can hear the final gospel call. These four judgments are so extensive that every mind on earth is forced to consider them. While people are considering the meaning of the judgments, they will be open to hear the everlasting gospel which contains an explanation of these judgments. As the people of earth contemplate the full gospel, they are invited to do something that most have never done - yield their lives to the truth contained in the Bible. The gospel clearly calls for obedience to the King of Kings. This is how the Bible becomes the center of a great controversy. This is why John says of the saints, they **"...obey God's commandments and remain faithful to Jesus."** Revelation 14:12 Satan, on the other hand, sees to it that circumstances will be so difficult that no one will be able to obey God's commandments unless they are willing to live by faith! The saints won't be able to buy or sell! Much more will be said about this in lessons 17-19. The point is that salvation will only come by faith and the saints will have the faith to obey!

Trust and obey

James clearly saw the true relationship between obedience and faith. He says, **"You see that a person is justified by what he does and not by faith alone. ...I will show you my faith by what I do."** James 2:24,18

So what moves God to send judgments upon peoples and nations? Notice what Jesus said to Isaiah, **"See, the Lord is going to lay waste the earth and devastate it; he will ruin its face and scatter its inhabitants... the earth will be completely laid waste and totally plundered. The Lord has spoken this word. The earth dries up and withers, and the world languishes and withers, the exalted of the earth languish. The earth is defiled by its people; they have disobeyed the laws, violated the statutes and broken the everlasting covenant. Therefore a curse consumes the earth; its people must bear their guilt. Therefore earth's inhabitants are burned up, and very few are left."** Isaiah 24:1-6

Isaiah was well aware of the hardness of people's hearts. He said, **"...When your judgments come upon the earth, the people of the world learn righteousness. Though grace is shown to the wicked, they do not learn righteousness; even in a land of uprightness they go on doing evil and regard not the majesty of the Lord."** Isaiah 26:9,10

Jesus loves mercy and He loves justice

Jesus holds each person accountable for their deeds. When people get away with murder, lying, stealing and cheating, evil rapidly grows. It's like nuclear fission. It's a chain reaction that can't be stopped. The runaway result is that sin spreads until almost every person is controlled or contaminated with it. When people, cities, nations or even the world reaches a point where love has no redeeming effect, Jesus sets His mercy aside and steps in with redeeming judgments. These judgments are sent to arouse people with the sinfulness of their course!

Ezekiel 14:12-27 gives a very clear explanation of the four judgments used in the fourth seal. **"The word of the Lord came to me: 'Son of man, if a country sins against me by being unfaithful and I stretch out my hand against it to cut off its food supply and send famine upon it and kill its men and their animals, even if these three men - Noah, Daniel and Job were in it, they could save only themselves by their righteousness, declares the Sovereign Lord.**

Or if I send wild beasts through that country and they leave it childless and it becomes desolate so that no one can pass through it because of the beasts.... Or if I bring a sword against that country and say, 'Let the sword pass throughout the land'... Or if I send a plague into that land and pour out my wrath upon it through bloodshed, killing its men and their animals...

How much worse will it be when I send against Jerusalem my four dreadful judgments - sword and famine and wild beasts and plague; to kill its men and their animals. Yet there will be some survivors - sons and daughters who will be brought out of it. They will come to you, and when you see their conduct and their actions, you will be consoled regarding the disaster I have brought upon Jerusalem - every disaster I have brought upon it... for you will know that I have done nothing in it without cause." Ezekiel 14:12-23

Notice the prophecy of Hosea: "The days of punishment are coming, the days of reckoning are at hand... because your sins are so many and your hostility so great, the prophet is considered a fool, the inspired man a maniac." Hosea 9:7

Through Moses, God warned the Israelites, **"If you obey the Lord your God and keep his commands and decrees that are written... the Lord thy God shall bless you in the land you are entering to possess. But if your heart turns away, and you are not obedient, and if you are drawn away to bow down to other gods and worship them... you will certainly be destroyed..."** Deuteronomy 30:10-18

New Testament warnings

If you think that the above warnings only apply to Old Testament days, consider the following warnings from the New Testament:

Peter said, **"For if God did not spare angels when they sinned, but sent them to hell, (the Greek word translated hell is "tartarosas" - the Greek equivalent to the bottomless pit), putting them into gloomy dungeons to be held for judgment; if he did not spare the ancient world when he brought the flood on its ungodly people, but protected Noah, a preacher of righteousness, and seven others; if he condemned the cities of Sodom and Gomorrah by burning them to ashes, and made them an example of *what is going to***

happen **to the ungodly... the Lord knows how to rescue godly men... and to hold the unrighteous for the day of judgment."** II Peter 2:4-9

Revelation says, **"...Come out of her (Babylon), my people, so that you will not share in her sins, so that you will not receive any of her plagues; for her sins are piled up to heaven, and God has remembered her crimes... Therefore in one day her plagues will overtake her: death, mourning and famine. She will be consumed by fire, for mighty is the Lord God who judges her."** Revelation 18:4,5,8

John says, **"I saw in heaven another great and marvelous sign: seven angels with the seven last plagues - last, because with them God's wrath is completed."** Revelation 15:1

From the above examples, it is evident that God has sent and will send judgments upon the world either in an effort to save or to punish. We need to notice two specific points.

First: In the case of corporate judgments (judgments upon groups of people), God initially offered mercy to those who would turn from wrong. In Noah's day, the ark was open to whomsoever would get on board. In Sodom and Gomorrah, God couldn't even find ten righteous people, but did save Lot and some of his family. In Jericho, the harlot

Rahab and her family were saved. In Nineveh, the entire city was saved through repentance!

While cities, nations and earth itself

The balance between divine justice and divine mercy is divine love.

may fill up their cups of iniquity, God seeks to save those who love Him and spares them from His judgments. II Peter 3:9 says that, **"(Jesus) is patient with you, not wanting anyone to perish, but everyone to come to repentance!"** This is divine mercy.

Secondly: God sends judgments upon people when their wicked acts take them *beyond* redeeming love. It is important to understand that there is a point of NO return where divine mercy is no longer available. It can be called the point of no return, the unpardonable sin or the close of probation (mercy). A person, city, nation and even earth itself can commit the unpardonable sin! When this point is reached, destruction follows.

Consider this interesting verse from Revelation 16:5,6: **"Then I heard the angel in charge of the waters say: 'You are just in these judgments, you who are and who were, the Holy One, because you have so judged; for they have shed the blood of your saints and prophets,** **and you have given them blood to drink as they deserve.' "**

The context of this verse is found during the seven last plagues which are yet future. In this text, an angel has just poured out one of the seven *last* plagues upon earth. More will be said about these horrible plagues later; but for now, it is important to notice that the angels, impartial observers of human conduct, declare God to be true and righteous for having punished humans in this manner! "Here is divine justice," the third angel exclaims. We ask, "how can this be?" The balance between divine mercy and divine justice is divine love.

This is a hard thing to understand at times. How can God be all merciful, all forgiving, and yet be able to execute punishment?

Review the reasons for judgments

Judgments are not pleasurable acts to God. The Bible calls them, "His strange work." See Isaiah 28:21. Why then does He send them? *God sends punishments upon people or nations for at least two reasons:*

First: He tries to bring evil-doers to repentance through warnings. But if the warnings go unheeded, He sends destruction to sober evil doers. If they defiantly refuse to turn from their evil, a point is finally reached where mercy is no longer meaningful. In fact, extended mercy only allows evil, violence and suffering to needlessly continue.

Some argue that the God of the Old Testament is not the same God described in the New Testament. This is not true! Jesus is always the same, yesterday, today and tomorrow (see Malachi 3:6 and Hebrews 1:10-12). He is longsuffering, yet, as in the eviction of Satan and his angels from heaven, (Ezekiel 28:14-17, Revelation 12:7,9) Jesus has clearly demonstrated that even in heaven there is a point where mercy becomes meaningless and justice must prevail.

As said earlier, Satan would have us misunderstand God's love. He would have us picture God as either a vengeful tyrant that zaps those who disagree with Him or a God that does not concern Himself with our sins. Either concept is wrong. The first concept is the foundation of the doctrine of an eternally burning hell. The second concept is the basis for amoral and decadent behavior. Those who understand that they will meet their Maker and have to give account for their deeds, are careful with their actions!

Secondly: God sends judgments upon earth to get man's attention. People forget God. They forget He owns the universe. We can forget that God means exactly what He says. Satan leads the world to distort or magnify God's patience incorrectly. His long-suffering is taken for granted and sinners become bold in their acts of sin (see Ecclesiastes 8:11 and Zephaniah 1:12). We may forget or even deny that judgments and justice eventually come, but the Bible record is not obscure on this matter. The fate of Sodom and Gomorrah, Jericho, and the people who lived before the Flood prove that God rises up when sin reaches an intolerable level.

The tribulation begins with opening of fourth seal.

The final test of mankind involves a time of great tribulation. Jesus spoke to his disciples about the magnitude of these judgments at the end of the world. He said, **"For there shall be great tribulation such as was not since the beginning of the world to this time, no, nor ever shall be."** Matthew 24:21 The time of trouble grows with intensity too. When the seven last plagues occur, it is tribulation beyond our comprehension. Daniel says, **"...There will be a time of distress such as has not happened from the beginning of nations until then."** Daniel 12:1

Revelation clearly predicts and describes the coming events that comprise the great tribulation. We are not left to guess what the trouble is or why it comes. As you can now understand, global trouble begins with the opening of the fourth seal!

The seven trumpets

Revelation does not leave us in darkness wondering how the final events occur! The total destruction caused under the fourth seal amounts to a total of fourteen events. These events are described as seven trumpets (or seven first plagues) and seven last plagues. Each plague has a special purpose and meaning.

A time of wrath

Before we look at the contents of the seven trumpets, we need to understand that the time period following the opening of the fourth seal until the arrival of Jesus in the sixth seal is appropriately called, "a time of wrath." Remember Gabriel's visit with Daniel? Review what Gabriel said, **"...I am going to tell you what will happen later in the time of wrath, because the vision concerns the appointed time of the end."** Daniel 8:19 On a later visit with Daniel, Gabriel told Daniel that Satan would appear in person upon earth! He said, **"The king (Satan) will do as he pleases. He will**

Six seals are opened between 1844 and the second coming.

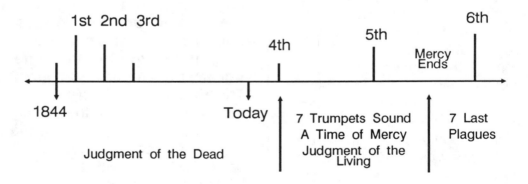

The seven seals reveal who Jesus really is. The seven trumpets awaken the world to its need of Jesus and the everlasting gospel tells how to receive Jesus and avoid the mark of the beast!

exalt and magnify himself above every god and will say unheard-of things against the God of gods. He will be successful until the time of wrath is completed, for what has been determined must take place." Daniel 11:36

The time of wrath is mentioned twice in Daniel's vision and John saw it too! Compare Daniel's verses above with Revelation 15:1. John says, **"I saw in heaven another great and marvelous sign: seven angels with the seven last plagues - last, because with them God's wrath is completed."** In other words, God's wrath is completed or fulfilled during the seven last plagues!

Study the chart and notice that the trumpets mark a time period of redemptive judgments because mercy is mixed with them. This underscores the purpose of the trumpets to awaken and arouse people to the sinfulness of their course, and to prepare them for the close of mercy.

Back to the sanctuary and the Day of Atonement

The time period of the seven trumpets marks the judgment of the living. We have studied the importance of the Day of Atonement in the wilderness. The Day of Atonement was the most important day in the Jewish year for the 10th day of the 7th month marked the close of Israel's judgment for that year.

To warn the Jews of this final and most important day of the year, the Feast of Trumpets began nine days earlier - on the 1st day of the seventh month (see Leviticus 23:24). Each day, according to the Talmud, trumpets sounded throughout the camp announcing the closing of mercy. On the 10th day, the actual Day of Atonement, the trumpets blasted throughout the land (see Leviticus 25:9) to signify that probation had ended.

The close of judgment was not a surprise in the wilderness and neither will it be a surprise to those living upon earth. In fact, Jesus is desirous that the close of probation come upon earth with ample warning so that all necessary preparations can be made by any desiring eternal life!

A clarion call

The Bible uses the trumpet as a symbol of warning or announcement. Notice the following references:

"Blow the trumpet in Zion; sound the alarm on my holy hill. Let all who live in the land tremble, for the day of the Lord is coming. It is close at hand." Joel 2:1

"I appointed watchmen over you and said 'Listen to the sound of the trumpet!'... I am bringing dis-

aster on this people, the fruit of their schemes, because they have not listened to my words and have rejected my law." Jeremiah 6:17,19

"...if anyone hears the trumpet but does not take warning and the sword comes and takes his life, his blood will be on his own head." Ezekiel 33:4

When Jesus returns, He will use the trumpet to announce His appearing! "...for the trumpet will sound, the dead will be raised imperishable, and we will all be changed." I Corinthians 15:52

Since ancient times, the trumpet has not only been an instrument of music, it has been a means of communication. For example, generals in battle directed their armies with trumpets. The trumpet was ideal because its penetrating sound could rise above the din of war or pierce the dark of night. Night watchmen were required to sound the trumpet if the enemy approached. Specific tunes were used to indicate assignment and signals. The apostle Paul says: "..if the trumpet does not sound a clear call, who will get ready for battle?" (I Corinthians 14:8).

So it will be. The sounding of the seven trumpets will be a clarion call. The seven trumpets of Revelation are symbols of warning or announcement. Their purpose is to awaken the world with the fact that

Jesus is about to appear. Their message is, "Get ready! Get ready! Get ready!" Since the trumpet is the loudest of all musical instruments and the number seven is usually considered to be a full or comprehensive number, these trumpets have global application. After all, God wants to awaken and arouse all people of Earth that Jesus is coming back to Earth to gather up those whose names are written in the book of life!

What takes place as each trumpet sounds?

1. Hail and fire mixed with blood. A third of the earth, trees, and all green grass is burned up. Revelation 8:7
2. A third of the sea is turned to blood, a third of the sea creatures die, and a third of the ships are destroyed. Revelation 8:8,9
3. A third of the rivers and the springs of waters turn bitter, and many people die from the waters. The name of this plague is "Wormwood" or bitterness. Revelation 8:10,11
4. One third of the sun, moon and stars are struck, and they turn dark. A third of the day will be without light, also a third of the night. Revelation 8:12
5. The angel king of the bottomless pit is let out. He brings a terrible affliction for five

months upon those who rebel against God. The torment is so bad that, **"men will seek death, but will not find it; they will long to die, but death will elude them."** See Revelation 9:1-12

6. Satan conducts a great war to conquer the world. Four angels at the great river Euphrates are released to kill a third of mankind. The number of troops will be myriads. These angels had been kept ready for this very hour, day, month and year! Revelation 9:13-19

7. Jesus concludes His special work in the heavenly sanctuary. There is an earthquake, lightning, rumblings, peals of thunder, and a great hailstorm. Revelation 11:15-19

The fourth seal opens and the first trumpet sounds

Jesus opens the fourth seal and initiates the great tribulation upon the world by sounding the trumpets. These warning plagues fall in response to our unrestrained evil and hardness of heart. **"...why has the Lord decreed such a great disaster against us? What wrong have we done? What sin have we committed against the Lord our God?... '(Your) houses are full of deceit; (you) have become rich and powerful and have grown fat and sleek. (Your) evil deeds have**

no limit.' " Jeremiah 16:10; 5:27,28

Thus the opening of the fourth seal will attract the attention of everyone on earth that God's wrath has broken out upon earth. These trumpet plagues are not man-made rather, these will be rightly called, "Acts of God" and will be correctly recognized as such. As in the days of Pharaoh, God says the world will know, **"I am the Lord that do these things."** See Exodus 7:5

Summary

From the Bible we have seen that Jesus has sent judgments upon the world in times past. Judgments from heaven come with warning. Jesus uses judgments to awaken and arouse people with the sinfulness of their course. His judgments can be redemptive or punitive. They can be a means of salvation or a means of destruction.

The opening of the fourth seal marks the beginning of the tribulation that is coming upon the earth. At the close of mercy, an even greater tribulation comes upon the earth in the form of seven last plagues! Daniel 12:1

Our next lesson will closely investigate each of the seven trumpets. The effects will be world wide. The awakening will be unlike anything ever seen on earth. The people of earth will be awakened to hear a very sobering message!

Quiz

1. What is the strongest evidence that the fourth seal hasn't opened yet?

2. Give an example of corporate punishment.

3. Name three of the seven religious systems of the world.

4. Can man be saved by works? Can man be saved by assuming he is saved? How is a person saved?

5. Why is Jesus going to send seven trumpets?

Notes:

The Seven Trumpets Part II

Lesson 15

Review

Our previous study surveyed the tribulation that marks the end of the world. From Daniel 8 and 11, we learned this time-period is referred to as "a time of wrath." We will understand the importance of this term more fully in this lesson.

In effect, the trumpets are designed to arrest the attention of the world so that everyone can hear the gospel. What is called "gospel" today is only a portion of the full gospel! Jesus clearly says that everyone is to hear the gospel, "and then the end will come." Matthew 24:14 The full gospel story hasn't been told to the world yet for the gospel must clearly explain Revelation's story! The full gospel story contains an explanation of the trumpets, the seals, the seven last plagues and the two beasts of Revelation.

John clearly saw that the remnant would have to give the gospel *again* to the world! See Revelation 10:8-11. The reason the gospel must go again throughout the world, is that in final form, the full gospel contains a special message from Revelation. This timely message not only explains the purpose of the trumpets, it gives a call to worship God. The call to worship God contains a very important test that affects the whole world! The everlasting gospel will separate those who really love God from those who hate the light of truth. Those who are now living up to all the light they have will rejoice and move forward with the greater light of the full gospel that is soon to light up every corner of the world!

Seven trumpets begin

Carefully read the following verses from Revelation:

"And I saw the seven angels who stand before God, and to them were given seven trumpets.

Another angel, who had a golden censer, came and stood at the altar. He was given much incense to offer, with the prayers of all the saints, on the golden altar before the throne. The smoke of the incense, together with the prayers of the saints, went up before God from the angel's hand. Then the angel took the censer, filled it with fire from the altar, and hurled it on the earth; and there came peals of thunder, rumblings, flashes of lightning and an earthquake. Then the seven angels who had the seven trumpets prepared to sound them." Revelation 8:2-6

A number of important things stand out in these verses. We will study two of them. First, observe the chronological sequence. Notice that the seven angels who stand before God are given seven trumpets THEN; the angel at the golden altar (of incense) hurls down a censer and THEN; there is thunder, rumblings, lightning and an earthquake and THEN; the seven angels prepare to sound their trumpets.

Secondly, notice that the angel at the altar places much incense on the altar before the trumpets sound.

What do these things mean?

As demonstrated in the previous lesson, the purpose of the trumpets is to awaken and arouse the world to hear the everlasting gospel. The throwing down of the censer and the commotion that follows on earth simultaneously marks the **beginning** of the trumpet sequence and the **end** of an atonement process in heaven. This process, like the great Day of Atonement, has an earthly sanctuary equivalent too. In ancient times, it was known as the "daily or continual" offering. Each morning and evening, a sacrifice was offered on the altar of burnt offering. This sacrifice was offered on behalf of the camp of Israel and not for any particular individual. In other words, this sacrifice was a corporate

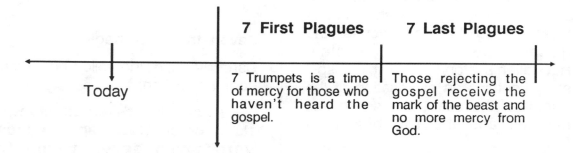

4th Seal opens when censer is thrown down

Today

7 First Plagues — 7 Trumpets is a time of mercy for those who haven't heard the gospel.

7 Last Plagues — Those rejecting the gospel receive the mark of the beast and no more mercy from God.

sacrifice. (See Numbers 15:22-31 for a clear distinction between corporate and individual sacrifices.)

In Israel's day, the morning and evening sacrifices provided corporate atonement on a continual or daily basis. This atonement was necessary so that Israel could dwell in God's consuming presence. Without atonement morning and evening, the camp of Israel could not exist! In a similar manner, Jesus has been interceding on behalf of the world since His ascension. A guilty race has been sheltered from the righteous justice of God through the daily or continual merits of Jesus' intercession. Just before the seven trumpets begin, the censer in heaven is thrown down indicating the sudden end of corporate intercession.

A sinful and defiled world will reap a terrible harvest. As in the days of Noah, earth in a corporate sense, will reach a point of no return. When this point is reached the wrath of Jesus will be exercised. The fourth seal will be opened and the predicted destruction will begin. The first four trumpets are warning judgments sent to the world saying, "Get ready, get ready. Prepare to meet your Maker."

Much incense

The angel at heaven's altar was given much incense to put on the altar before the 7 trumpets sound. This fragrance of incense along with the prayers of the saints goes up before God. What does this mean?

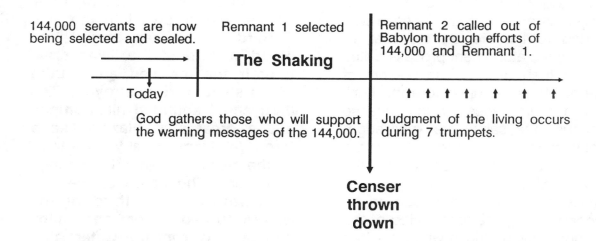

144,000 servants are now being selected and sealed.

Today

God gathers those who will support the warning messages of the 144,000.

Remnant 1 selected

The Shaking

Remnant 2 called out of Babylon through efforts of 144,000 and Remnant 1.

Judgment of the living occurs during 7 trumpets.

Censer thrown down

144,000 + Remnants 1 and 2 = Great Harvest

In the wilderness sanctuary, a special incense was offered before the Lord each morning and evening as the daily sacrifice was being applied. Exodus 30:7,8,37 On the Day of Atonement, the high priest carried a censer full of burning coals with two handfuls of this incense into the Most Holy Place. Jesus said, **"He (the high priest) is to put the incense on the fire before the Lord, and the smoke of the incense will conceal the atonement cover above the Testimony (the ark of the Testimony), so that he will not die."** Leviticus 16:13 That which separated the high priest from the consuming glory of God was only a veil of smoke!

From Revelation 8:5 we conclude that the censer is thrown down because its service is finished. The daily atonement conducted by this censer is ended. Extra incense was added to the fire on the altar to sustain the atonement process a little longer than usual. The prayers of the saints come up before the Lord with the fragrance of the incense because the saints are knowledgeable, ready and prepared for the hour of trial that occurs during the trumpets. The judgment day of God has come. The first people to be judged during the time-period of the trumpets will be those who have had an opportunity to prepare for these things! 1 Peter 4:17

This point brings up the issue of the 144,000 which will be studied later. For now, study the diagram on the preceding page to understand how the 144,000 and their support group (called "remnant 1" in this seminar) are prepared to go throughout the world during the time period of the seven trumpets to gather in the remaining children of God (identified as "remnant 2" in this seminar) which are in Babylon.

The first 3 trumpets

"The first angel sounded his trumpet, and there came hail and fire mixed with blood, and it was hurled down upon the earth. A third of the earth was burned up, a third of the trees were burned up, and all the green grass was burned up. The second angel sounded his trumpet, and something like a huge mountain, all ablaze, was thrown into the sea. A third of the sea turned into blood, a third of the living creatures in the sea died, and a third of the ships were destroyed. The third angel sounded his trumpet, and a great star, blazing like a torch, fell from the sky on a third of the rivers and on the springs of water. The name of the star is Wormwood. A third of the waters turned bitter, and many people died from the waters that had become bitter." Revelation 8:7-11

Perhaps the first three trumpets are caused by our earth's orbit passing through an asteroid belt. The presence of these dangerous belts in our galaxy has been known for many years. In fact, the rings about the planet Saturn are rings of asteroids. An asteroid is a piece of cosmic debris that can range in size from a golf ball to several miles in diameter.

At the annual meeting of the American Geophysical Union in December, 1989, Clark Chapman of the Planetary Science Institute in Tucson, Arizona, and David Morrison, chief of the space science division at NASA's Ames Research Center in Mountain View, California, shocked their audience of 4,000 scientists by suggesting that, "the risk of death from a wandering asteroid from outer space is somewhat greater than the risk of an individual American dying in an airplane crash." Their calculations are based on the fact that more than 100 major meteors have recently impacted the surface of the moon. In March of 1989, a half-mile wide asteroid came within 500,000 miles of Earth. If it had hit the earth, astronomers said, "it would have crashed with enough violence to destroy a good-sized country."

John's description of the first trumpet is a hail-storm, not of ice, but of fire! This fire burns up a third of the land and trees and all the green grass. Because the next two trumpets are caused by large meteors, this author believes the first trumpet

is caused by a large amount of cosmic debris such as baseball-size meteors which enter our atmosphere and impact the earth thus causing a large number of fires. Men will be powerless to stop the fires because there are so many and they are so scattered. The death and destruction described in this trumpet cannot be stopped.

When the second angels sounds his trumpet, John saw a large meteor, perhaps a mile in diameter, hit the sea. The effect is immediate. The resulting tidal wave destroys a third of the ships! The toxins released by the intense heat of the meteor and the vaporizing of the oxygen within the water destroys a third of the marine life. Perhaps the "blood" John saw is the red tide that overtakes deoxygenated water.

When the third angel sounds his trumpet, a large meteor hits a continent or land mass. Perhaps an instantaneous series of earthquakes follows to redistribute tectonic forces far beneath the surface of the earth. The movement of tectonic plates collapses thousands of water wells that provide cities with drinking water. What drinking water is available is contaminated by sewage, refuse and toxic waste that has been buried. Many people die from drinking the water.

Note that each of the first three trumpets affects 1/3 of whatever they fall upon. If we add together the 1/3 of each trumpet, this could mean that 3/3 or all of the earth will be affected by these trumpets. This would be consistent with the idea that all the world must be awakened to hear the gospel message. We don't know just how earth was represented to John in this vision. Maybe 1/3 of the area he was viewing was affected or perhaps, 1/3 of the total earth was affected. Either way, the result of the first three trumpets is awful.

The student may be somewhat skeptical of the first three trumpets occurring as a result of meteorites. Such skepticism is respected. For further study on this subject, read the June, 1989 issue of *National Geographic Magazine*. *National Geographic* features an article on this interesting subject titled, "Extinctions." The hypothesis of this article is that mass extinctions occurred in the distant past due to large meteors impacting the earth. (The face of the moon clearly reveals a history of many large meteoric impacts.) Scientists are quite confident that large meteors have impacted the earth in the past and they speculate that dinosaurs became extinct because of them. What is so ironic is that while scientists are studying the past, the Bible predicts mass extinctions in the **future** in this very fashion!

Rick Gore, the author of the *National Geographic* article wrote, "Most scientists now concur that at least one great extraterrestrial object struck the planet around the time the dinosaurs died out... The idea that large objects could strike our planet and cause mass extinctions was considered radical until just a decade ago. Then a team of researchers at the University of California found high levels of iridium - a metal rare on earth but common in meteorites - in a thin layer of clay laid down about the time dinosaurs became extinct. Their conclusion - that an asteroid hit earth 66 million years ago, wreaking environmental havoc - shocked the scientific world. Further analysis of the iridium layer has supported the impact, although scientists are widely divided over its effects." Ibid, page 665, 666.

Perhaps very large meteors have impacted this planet in the past. A number of craters clearly seem to indicate such impacts. (The largest in North America is in Manson, Iowa. It's about 18 miles wide.) What is so interesting about the scientific pursuit of this idea, is that scientists have created computer models of what could happen if a large meteor hit the sea or hit the land. See if you notice any parallels from *National Geographic* and John's description in Revelation: "A huge plume would push the atmosphere aside... Winds of hundreds of kilometers an hour would sweep the planet for hours, drying trees like a giant hair dryer. Two-thousand degree rock vapor would spread rapidly. It would condense to white hot grains that could have started additional fires.... Volcanoes erupt, tsunamis crash into the continents. The sky grows dark for months, perhaps years... (water sources) become anoxic or toxic... creatures die." Ibid., page 673.

The fourth trumpet

"The fourth angel sounded his trumpet, and a third of the sun was struck, a third of the moon, and a third of the stars, so that a third of them turned dark. A third of the day was without light, and also a third of the night." Revelation 8:12

This trumpet obviously marks a phenomenal change in the heavens. Just how this is done, John doesn't say. Following the scenario in *National Geographic* the darkening of the sun, moon and stars could come as a result of the previous three trumpets. With the sun darkened, vegetation becomes stunted. Food crops which were wiped out as a result of the fires in the first trumpet, will not recover. The prospects of life on Earth after the first four trumpets sound will not be heartening.

As the people of earth witness these terribly awesome things, they will be desperate about survival. In their suffering, they will seek the meaning of these events. Clearly, these calamities are "acts of God."

Regardless of religious belief or cultural background, each person will be alarmed and interested. As people begin to compare the first four trumpets with the story of Revelation, the truthfulness and meaning of Revelation's story will blossom. Thus the minds of people in every nation, kindred, tongue and people will be opened to hear a prophetic explanation of what these events are all about. In short, people everywhere will be anxious to hear the everlasting gospel!

Now, three curses

As if the asteroids weren't bad enough, the next three trumpets are even more powerful. John says, **"As I watched, I heard an eagle that was flying in midair call out in a loud voice: 'Woe! Woe! Woe to the inhabitants of the earth, because of the trumpet blasts about to be sounded by the other three angels!' "** Revelation 8:13 This eagle is one of the four living creatures (senior angels) that John saw earlier. See Revelation 4:7. The message of this living creature is that the next three trumpets are curses. That is, they directly fall upon certain people and not the physical elements of earth.

Take a close look at the fifth trumpet

This trumpet marks the appearance of Satan claiming to be Jesus. He is the "angel king" of the Abyss. Notice John's description:

"The fifth angel sounded his trumpet, and I saw a star that had fallen from the sky to the earth. The star was given the key to the shaft of the Abyss. When he opened the Abyss, smoke rose from it like the smoke from a gigantic furnace. The sun and sky were darkened by the smoke from the Abyss.

And out of the smoke locusts came down upon the earth and were given power like that of scorpions of the earth.

They were told not to harm the grass of the earth or any plant or tree, but only those people who did not have the seal of God on their foreheads.

They were not given power to kill them, but only to torture them for five months. And the agony they suffered was like that of the sting of a scorpion when it strikes a man. During those days men will seek death, but will not find it; they will long to die, but death will elude them.

The locusts looked like horses prepared for battle. On their heads they wore something like crowns of gold, and their faces resembled human faces. Their hair was like women's hair, and their teeth were like lions' teeth. They had breastplates like breastplates of iron, and the sound of their wings was like the thundering of many horses and chariots rushing into battle.

They had tails and stings like scorpions, and in their tails they had power to torment people for five months. They had as king over them the angel of the Abyss, whose name in Hebrew is Abaddon, and in Greek, Apollyon. The first woe is past; two other woes are yet to come." Revelation 9:1-12

The language of this trumpet is generally analogous. John best describes the things he saw with analogies or with allusions to Old Testament references. Actually, the meaning of this trumpet is better understood when it is compared to Joel 2, for Joel saw a very similar scene. The difference between Joel and John is that John saw the coming of Satan (the angel king from the Abyss) while Joel saw the coming of the Lord! Notice Joel's remarks:

"Blow the trumpet in Zion; sound the alarm on my holy hill. Let all who live in the land tremble, *for the day of the Lord* is coming. It is close at hand - a day of darkness and gloom, a day of clouds and blackness.

Like dawn spreading across the mountains a large and mighty

army (of locusts) comes, such as never was of old nor ever will be in ages to come. Before them fire devours, behind them a flame blazes... nothing escapes them.

They have the appearance of horses; they gallop along like cavalry. With a noise like that of chariots they leap over the mountaintops...

At the sight of them, nations are in anguish, every face turns pale... Before them the earth shakes, the sky trembles, and the sun and moon are darkened, and the stars no longer shine.

The Lord thunders at the head of his army; his forces are beyond number, and mighty are those who obey his command. The day of the Lord is great; it is dreadful. Who can endure it?"   Joel 2:1-11

Compare their views

Joel saw a great army of locusts that looked like horses. John saw the same.

Joel saw the sun and moon darkened. John saw the same.

Joel marveled at the power of the army. John marveled at the same.

Joel saw the Lord at the head of His army. John saw the angel king of the Abyss at the head of his army.

Two important connecting points are presented regarding the appearing of Satan:

1.   Satan is let out of the Abyss (spirit world) in Revelation 9 and is returned to the Abyss in Revelation 20. **"And I saw an angel coming down out of heaven, having the key to the Abyss and holding in his hand a great chain. He seized the dragon, that ancient serpent, who is the devil, or Satan, and bound him for a thousand years. *He threw him into the Abyss* and locked and sealed it over him..."**   Revelation 20:1-3

2.   From the fifth trumpet we learn that Satan is allowed to come up out of the Abyss and physically appear upon earth during the fifth trumpet. What will he do after he appears? "They were told not to harm the grass of the earth or any plant or tree, but only those people who did not have the seal of God on their foreheads. They were not given power to kill them, but only to torture them for five months..." Revelation 9:4,5 It is interesting to note from these verses that Satan and his an-

gels cannot harm the physical things of earth that have been already hurt during the first trumpet.

Why do Satan and his angels torment the wicked and not the saints? To make the world violently angry with the Two Witnesses and their followers!

Two Witnesses have great power

We will study the Two Witnesses in our next lesson. For now, we need only to understand that they are God's representatives upon earth during the trumpets. They have great powers and the earth is afraid of them! Notice what John says about them, **"If anyone tries to harm them, fire comes from their mouths and devours their enemies. This is how anyone who wants to harm them must die. These men have power to shut up the sky so that it will not rain during the time they are prophesying; and they have power to turn the waters into blood and to strike the earth with every kind of plague as often as they want."** Revelation 11:5,6

Satan, after appearing upon earth torments the wicked beyond what the Two Witnesses have already done and lays the blame upon God's representatives. Thus the world becomes even more *enraged* with the Two Witnesses and their followers and concludes that they must be destroyed.

Who is the angel king, the beast from the Abyss?

Only once in Revelation's story does an "angel king" comes out of the Abyss. Twice in Revelation, a "beast" ascends out of the Abyss. Since Revelation 12:9 clearly tells us that the dragon-like beast is a fallen angel called Satan, we can safely say the "angel king" that ascends from the Abyss in chapter 9 is the devil. When we compare Joel's account of the second coming with the appearing of the angel king from the Abyss, we can be safe in concluding that Satan is the angel king.

What does the beast from the Abyss do? Notice the following verses: **"Now when they (the Two Witnesses) have finished their testimony, *the beast that comes up from the Abyss* will attack them, and overpower and kill them."** Revelation 11:7

"The beast which you saw... will come up out of the Abyss and go to his destruction. The inhabitants of the earth whose names have not been written in the book of life from the creation of the world will be astonished when they see the beast..." Revelation 17:8

When Satan appears on earth claiming to be God, the world will be astonished. He will almost deceive the entire world with his miracles and great supernatural powers. Satan will eventually "kill" the effectiveness of God's representatives by appearing to be so powerful and so much greater than those representing God's cause. Each person will have to make a very hard decision: follow the teachings of the Bible and receive the wrath of Satan or follow the teachings of Satan (claiming to be God) and receive the wrath of God.

Revelation 17:8 clearly says that those whose names *are not* written in the book of life will be astonished at the appearing of Satan. But the saints will be expecting him. After all, the fifth trumpet clearly explains when he appears. We'll study Satan's appearing and work more closely in a later lesson. For now, understand that he appears during the fifth trumpet.

A close look at the sixth trumpet

The second woe is a great war. John says, **"The sixth angel sounded his trumpet, and I heard a voice coming from the horns of the golden altar that is before God. It said to the sixth angel who had the trumpet, 'Release the four angels who are bound at the great river Euphrates.' And the four angels who had been kept ready for this very hour and day and month and year were released to kill a third of mankind.**

The number of the mounted troops was two hundred million. I heard their number. The horses and riders I saw in my vision looked like this: Their breastplates were fiery red, dark blue, and yellow as sulfur. The heads of the horses resembled the heads of lions, and out of their mouths came fire, smoke and sulfur.

A third of mankind was killed by the three plagues of fire, smoke and sulfur that came out of their mouths. The power of the horses was in their mouths and in their tails; for their tails were like snakes, having heads with which they inflict injury. The rest of mankind that were not killed by these plagues still did not repent of the work of their hands; they did not stop worshiping demons, and idols of gold, silver, bronze, stone and wood; idols that cannot see or hear or walk. Nor did they repent of their murders, their magic arts, their sexual immorality or their thefts. The second woe has passed; the third woe is coming soon." Revelation 9:13-21, 11:14

This trumpet describes a great war (the ultimate holy crusade) into which Satan leads his deceived followers. Satan sets out to establish a one-world government and he succeeds for a short time. Satan overcomes all political opposition and crushes the work of God upon earth. He, Satan, as God, will sit on a throne as King over the kings of earth, and Lord of lords over the religious systems of earth. He will rule the world through deception and force. Daniel saw the conclusion of this great war in his vision (Daniel 11:21-45). The outcome is that Satan appears to win. The war under the sixth seal, like any war, forces everyone to take sides. At last the world stands in two camps: those obeying Satan, and those obeying Jesus!

A close look at the final trumpet

Now comes the close of mercy. Everyone has made his decision. John says, **"The seventh angel sounded his trumpet, and there were loud voices in heaven, which said: 'The kingdom of the world has become the kingdom of our Lord and of his Christ, and he will reign for ever and ever.'**

And the twenty-four elders, who were seated on their thrones before God, fell on their faces and worshiped God, saying: 'We give thanks to you, Lord God Almighty, who is and who was, because you have taken your great power and have begun to reign. The nations were angry; and your wrath has come. The time has come for judging the dead, and for reward-
ing your servants the prophets and your saints and those who reverence your name, both small and great; and for destroying those who destroy the earth.'

Then God's temple in heaven was opened, and within his temple was seen the ark of his covenant. And there came flashes of lightning, rumblings, peals of thunder, an earthquake and a great hailstorm." Revelation 11:15-19

This trumpet announces the close of probation. Mercy has been extended as long as possible. Every person has made his decision for or against the gospel. Those who sided with Satan carry the mark of Satan - a mark necessary to conduct business, a permit to buy and sell! Those who sided with the gospel appear frail, weak and helpless against the dragon. They can't buy or sell. All forms of life-support are cut off. Satan has eliminated every means of earthly survival for them. In fact, the devil will lead the world in a united effort to exterminate these people as quickly as possible.

Jesus distracts the consolidated powers of Satan by sending the seven last plagues. This is the third woe or curse mentioned by the living creature. The awful and terrible plagues containing the fury of God's wrath fall upon all who received the mark of the beast.

Trumpets parallel 7 last plagues

There are some obvious comparisons between the trumpets and the plagues. Notice:

Seven trumpets

1. Hail, fire, and blood upon 1/3 of earth
2. One third of the sea turns to blood
3. One third of the drinking water becomes bitter
4. Sun, moon and stars affected (1/3 of heaven struck)
5. Satan appears bringing affliction on the wicked
6. Great War - millions killed
7. Hailstorm, earthquake

Seven last plagues

1. Terrible sores upon all rebelling against God
2. Sea turns to blood - everything in it dies
3. Drinking water and rivers turn to blood
4. Sun scorches people with intense heat
5. Great affliction on the government of Antichrist
6. Final war upon saints - Armageddon
7. Great hailstorm, earthquake and final destruction of earth

The point is made that the trumpets (seven first plagues) are samples in many respects of the seven last plagues. The main difference between these two groups of plagues is God's mercy.

Those that keep the commandments of God and remain faithful (faithful means faith-full) to Jesus will live by this precious promise: **"He who dwells in the shelter of the Most High will rest in the shadow of the Almighty. I will say of the Lord, 'He is my refuge and my fortress, my God, in whom I trust.' Surely he will save you from the fowler's snare and from the deadly pestilence. He will cover you with his feathers, and under his wings you will find refuge; his faithfulness will be your shield and rampart.**

You will not fear the terror of night, nor the arrow that flies by day, nor the pestilence that stalks in the darkness, nor the plague that destroys at midday. A thousand may fall at your side, ten thousand at your right hand, but it will not come near you. You will only observe with your eyes and see the punishment of the wicked.

If you make the Most High your dwelling - even the Lord, who is my refuge - then no harm will befall you, no disaster will come near your tent." Psalm 91:1-10

Summary

The seven trumpets will soon come as horrible and devastating judgments upon earth. Yet, it is the very nature of these things that arrests the world's attention to hear the everlasting gospel. Outside the context of such dramatic events, what credibility does the gospel have today among earth's 5.2 billion people?

The purpose of the trumpets is salvation, for the door to salvation remains open until the seventh trumpet sounds. Revelation's story will come into sharp focus when the trumpets begin because people all over the world will see things coming to pass right before their very eyes! Thus the full gospel will go the ends of the earth in a very short time period.

One final point, the trumpets are only "samples" of the wrath of God. The seven last plagues are even worse. If the trumpets are terrible, what will be the effect of the seven last plagues? The severity of these things should cause us to carefully consider the everlasting gospel for it contains a very specific warning! This warning will be studied in the next volume.

Quiz

1. What does the throwing down of the censer indicate?

2. What causes the destruction described in the first three trumpets?

3. What happens during the fifth trumpet?

4. What happens during the sixth trumpet?

5. What is the major difference between the trumpets and plagues?